DESIGNERS AND TEST PILOTS

TIME
LIFE ®
BOOKS

This volume is one of a series that traces the adventure and science of aviation, from the earliest manned balloon ascension through the era of jet flight.

DESIGNERS AND TEST PILOTS

by Richard P. Hallion

AND THE EDITORS OF TIME-LIFE BOOKS

TIME-LIFE BOOKS, ALEXANDRIA, VIRGINIA

Time-Life Books Inc.
is a wholly owned subsidiary of

TIME INCORPORATED

FOUNDER: Henry R. Luce 1898-1967

Editor-in-Chief: Henry Anatole Grunwald
President: J. Richard Munro
Chairman of the Board: Ralph P. Davidson
Executive Vice President: Clifford J. Grum
Editorial Director: Ralph Graves
Group Vice President, Books: Joan D. Manley

TIME-LIFE BOOKS INC.

EDITOR: George Constable
Executive Editor: George Daniels
Director of Design: Louis Klein
Board of Editors: Dale M. Brown, Thomas A. Lewis,
Martin Mann, Robert G. Mason, Ellen Phillips,
Gerry Schremp, Gerald Simons, Rosalind Stubenberg,
Kit van Tulleken
Director of Administration: David L. Harrison
Director of Research: Carolyn L. Sackett
Director of Photography: John Conrad Weiser

PRESIDENT: Reginald K. Brack Jr.
Executive Vice President: John Steven Maxwell
Vice Presidents: George Artandi, Stephen L. Bair,
Peter G. Barnes, Nicholas Benton, John L. Canova,
Beatrice T. Dobie, Christopher T. Linen, James L. Mercer,
Paul R. Stewart

THE EPIC OF FLIGHT

EDITORS: Dale M. Brown, Lee Hassig
Designer: Van W. Carney
Chief Researcher: W. Mark Hamilton

Editorial Staff for *Designers and Test Pilots*

Associate Editors: John Manners (text);
Jane N. Coughran (pictures)
Text Editor: Robert Menaker
Staff Writers: Kevin D. Armstrong, Deborah Berger-Turnbull,
Rachel Cox, Glenn Martin McNatt, Mark Steele
Researchers: LaVerle Berry, Barbara Brownell, Linda Lee,
Charles McCardell, Gregory McGruder, B. Jean Strong
Assistant Designer: Anne K. DuVivier
Copy Coordinators: Stephen G. Hyslop, Anthony K. Pordes
Art Assistant: Lorraine D. Rivard
Picture Coordinator: Renée DeSandies
Editorial Assistants: Constance B. Strawbridge,
Myrna E. Traylor

Special Contributors: Lydia Preston, Dana Bell

Editorial Operations
Design: Arnold C. Holeywell (assistant director); Anne B.
Landry (art coordinator); James J. Cox (quality control)
Research: Jane Edwin (assistant director), Louise D. Forstall
Copy Room: Susan Galloway Goldberg (director),
Celia Beattie
Production: Feliciano Madrid (director), Gordon E. Buck,
Peter Inchauteguiz

Correspondents: Elisabeth Kraemer (Bonn); Margot
Hapgood, Dorothy Bacon (London); Miriam Hsia, Lucy T.
Voulgaris (New York); Maria Vincenza Aloisi, Josephine du
Brusle (Paris); Ann Natanson (Rome). Valuable assistance
was also provided by: Helga Kohl, Angelika Lemmer (Bonn);
Brigid Graumann (Brussels); Judy Aspinall, Lesley Coleman
(London); Christina Lieberman (New York); Ann Wise
(Rome); ⌇⌇⌇ Ohyauchi (Tokyo).

THE AUTHOR

Dr. Richard P. Hallion is the historian of the
Air Force Flight Test Center at Edwards Air
Force Base, California. Formerly, Dr. Hallion
was Curator of Science and Technology and
of Space, Science and Exploration at the National
Air and Space Museum in Washington,
D.C. He is the author of *Test Pilots* and *Supersonic Flight*.

THE CONSULTANTS

Dr. Tom D. Crouch, the principal consultant,
is Curator of Aeronautics at the National Air
and Space Museum in Washington. He has
written several books and articles on the early
history of aviation, and is also an avid balloonist
in his spare time.

Dr. Howard S. Wolko, a specialist in aircraft
structures, is an Advisor on Technology and
Aeronautics at the National Air and Space
Museum. The author of numerous technical
papers and monographs, he also participated
in the development of several of the X-series
of experimental research airplanes.

For information about any Time-Life book, please write:
Reader Information
Time-Life Books
541 North Fairbanks Court
Chicago, Illinois 60611

Library of Congress Cataloguing in Publication Data
Hallion, Richard.
    Designers and test pilots.
    (The Epic of flight)
    Bibliography: p.
    Includes index.
    1. Airplanes—Design and construction—History.
2. Airplanes—Flight testing—History.   I. Time-Life
Books.   II. Title.   III. Series.
TL 671.2.H33 1983   629.134'1'09   83-7997
ISBN 0-8094-3316-8
ISBN 0-8094-3317-6 (lib. bdg.)

CONTENTS

A giant among aircraft designers

In September 1908, five years after the epochal flight at Kitty Hawk, the Wright brothers demonstrated a new plane at Fort Myer, Virginia. Orville Wright put the flying machine through its paces. As was customary for early designers, he was his own test pilot.

Among the onlookers was Donald Wills Douglas, a 16-year-old from Brooklyn. Like many who witnessed such flights, he was enthralled. But unlike those who simply wanted to fly, Douglas was determined to create airplanes.

Douglas entered the U.S. Naval Academy in 1909, but transferred three years later to the Massachusetts Institute of Technology to study aeronautics, turning himself into one of the nation's first aeronautical engineers. He began as an aircraft designer for the Glenn L. Martin Company, but by 1920 Douglas was ready to start his own business.

Backed by an aviation enthusiast named David Davis, he founded the Davis-Douglas Company in the back room of a Los Angeles barbershop. Davis soon lost interest in the venture, but over the next two decades the company expanded to become one of the world's largest airplane manufacturers, turning out such highly regarded military aircraft as the Navy's DT-1 torpedo plane and the Army's Douglas World Cruiser *(pages 12-13)*. Douglas never had to test his own planes. By his time, he could call on the services of professional test pilots—skilled aviators who methodically explored the potential of untried aircraft.

In 1932, Douglas designers turned their talents to building a commercial airliner. The result in 1933 was a prototype called the DC-1. From it came the DC-2 and in 1935 one of the most successful passenger planes ever—the DC-3. Unprecedented in durability, performance and comfort, the DC-3 would make air travel commonplace.

But this triumph did not belong to Douglas alone. The DC-3 embodied the accumulated knowledge of an entire generation of designers in the United States and Europe, pioneers like Germany's Hugo Junkers, Britain's Geoffrey de Havilland and America's Jack Northrop. In years to come, men like them—and a handful of courageous test pilots—would expand the realm of flight to the very edge of space and to velocities six times the speed of sound.

At the beginning of his career as a designer, Douglas displays two wing ribs typical of the day. A row of such ribs, connected by horizontal spars and covered with fabric, made up a wing. The background diagrams on these and the following pages are from the original blueprint of the DC-2.

Midshipman Douglas visits Norway on a training cruise.

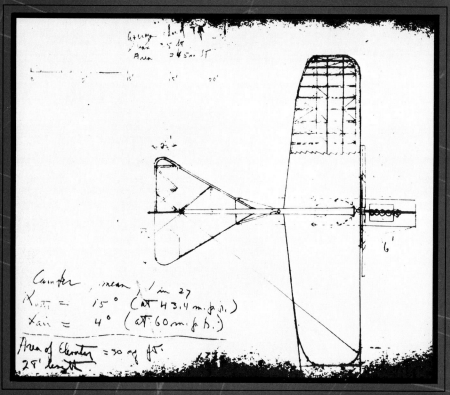

Douglas drew this "aquaeroplane" in 1912, the year he left Annapolis. "It was merely a sketch of what I then thought a seaplane should be," he recalled years later.

One of Douglas' earliest efforts—a 1909 rubber-band-powered plane with twin propellers—dominates the young designer's dormitory room. Douglas test-flew his model aircraft in the cavernous Naval Academy armory.

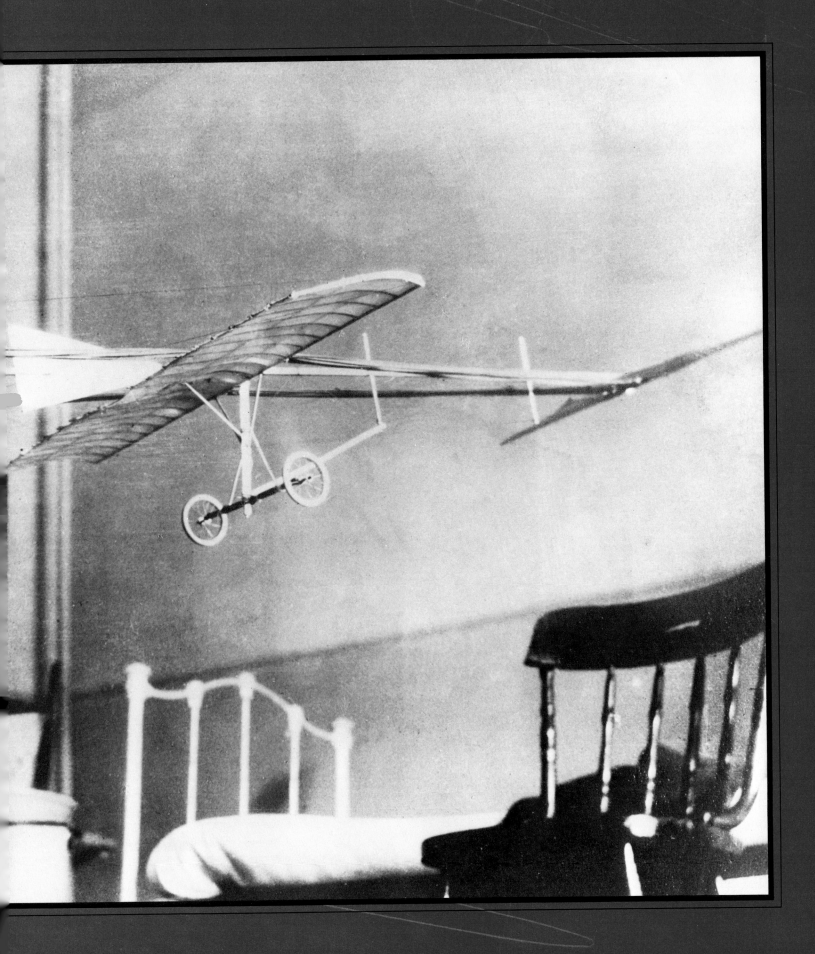

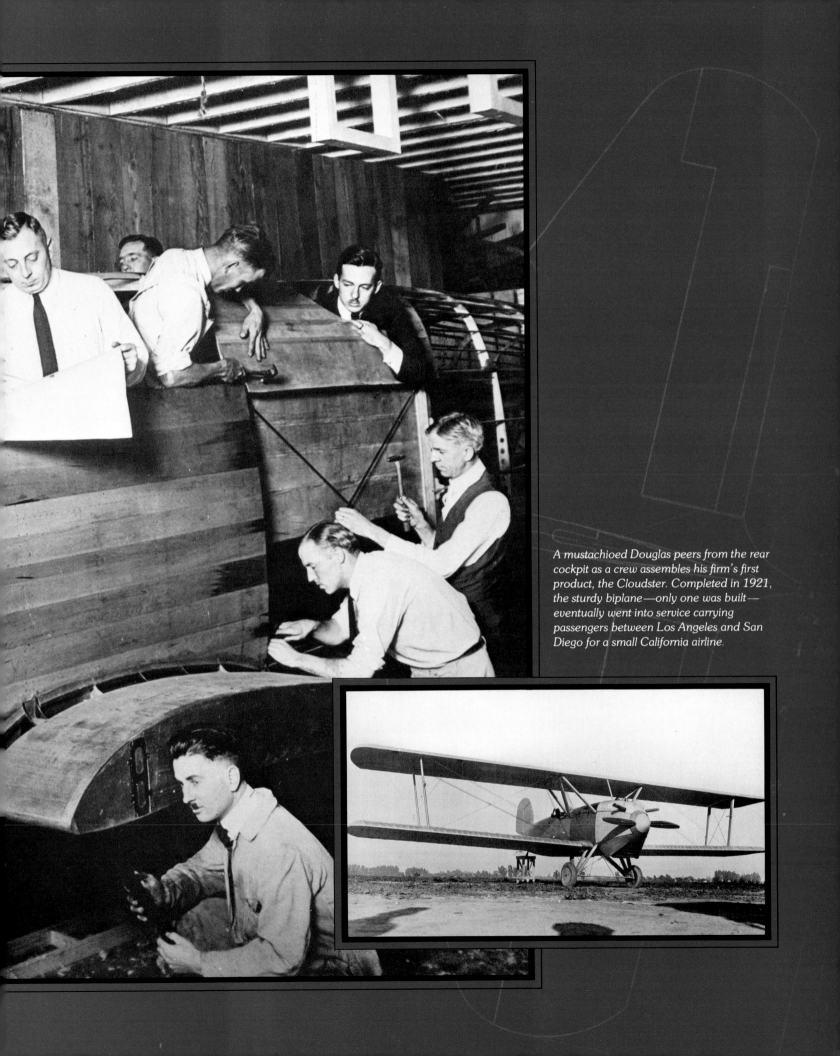

A mustachioed Douglas peers from the rear cockpit as a crew assembles his firm's first product, the Cloudster. Completed in 1921, the sturdy biplane—only one was built— eventually went into service carrying passengers between Los Angeles and San Diego for a small California airline.

Taking delivery of the first DT-1 torpedo plane in 1921, a Navy lieutenant shakes hands with test pilot Eric Springer as Douglas—sporting a checked cap—looks on. Based on the design of the Cloudster, the DT-1 was the first of Douglas' many lucrative projects for the military.

A Douglas Dolphin, its landing gear tucked up beside its metal hull, cruises over San Francisco Bay in 1932. Conceived as a luxury "air yacht," the amphibian found few private buyers in the economically depressed '30s, but the U.S. armed forces used it as a transport and coastal patrol craft.

Four Douglas World Cruisers, commissioned by the Army for an attempt to fly around the world, prepare to leave Santa Monica, California, for Seattle, Washington, and the official start of the trip. The success of the 1924 circumnavigation gave Douglas its boastful motto: "First around the world."

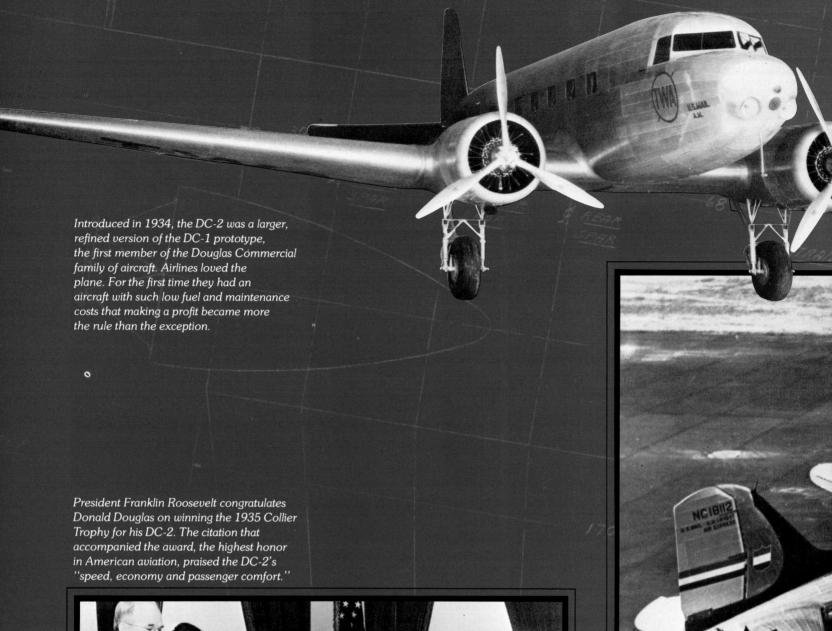

Introduced in 1934, the DC-2 was a larger,
refined version of the DC-1 prototype,
the first member of the Douglas Commercial
family of aircraft. Airlines loved the
plane. For the first time they had an
aircraft with such low fuel and maintenance
costs that making a profit became more
the rule than the exception.

President Franklin Roosevelt congratulates
Donald Douglas on winning the 1935 Collier
Trophy for his DC-2. The citation that
accompanied the award, the highest honor
in American aviation, praised the DC-2's
"speed, economy and passenger comfort."

As a crowd looks on, passengers board a United Air Lines DC-3 in the late 1930s. By 1942, 80 per cent of the planes flown by America's scheduled airlines were DC-3s.

Janvier 1913. 50 centimes 9me année. — No 1.

La Revue Sportive Illustrée

ORGANE OFFICIEL

Rédacteur en Chef :
Chevalier Jules de THIER
5, Rue du Casque
LIÉGE
Téléphone 3345

des Automobiles Clubs d'Anvers, de Bruges, des Flandres, de Liége, de Namur-Luxembourg, d'Ostende et du littoral, de Spa, de Verviers, du Royal Golf-Club de Belgique, des Aéro-Clubs de Liége-Spa d'Ostende et du littoral, du Cercle Equestre Gantois, de la Société Hippique de Liége, du Royal Sport Hippique d'Anvers, de la Société Royale Nautique Anversoise, du Royal Yacht Club d'Ostende, du Motor Yacht Club de Belgique, du Royal Sailing Club, du Modèle Yacht Club d'Anvers, de l'Antwerp Motor Club, de la Société Royale de Tir aux Pigeons d'Ostende, etc.

Correspondants pour la France : Charles FAROUX et Jacques MORTANE

Directeur :
Ernest VAN HAMMÉE
9, Rue Scailquin, 9
BRUXELLES
Téléphone A 7702

Le Triomphateur de l'Année

La plus belle épreuve d'aviation de l'année écoulée fut sans nul doute la classique Coupe Gordon Bennett qui se courut à Chicago devant deux cent mille spectateurs Elle fut l'occasion d'un nouveau triomphe pour les "Monocoques,, Deperdussin qui finirent en tête Et son glorieux vainqueur, Jules Védrines, en ramenant en France le glorieux trophée, lui assure, pour 1913, un succès sans précédent. Notre photographie représente le "Monocoque,, Deperdussin que l'on peut admirer au Salon de Bruxelles. Dans le médaillon, M. A. Deperdussin à qui l'on doit, en partie, le triomphe actuel de l'aviation

1

A dangerous age of trial and error

In the May 6, 1911, issue of *Flight,* one of Britain's leading aviation journals, there appeared a small advertisement addressed to inventors.

"Why break your Aeroplane yourself," it read, "when we do it for you?" The advertiser, a personable 22-year-old named Wilfred Parke, was attempting to cast himself in the role of test pilot for the handful of Britons who were constructing flying machines of their own design. Perhaps the designers were put off by the ad's breezy jocularity. Or perhaps they somehow learned that the would-be test flier had acquired his pilot's license only two weeks earlier and had started learning to fly just two weeks before that. Whatever the reason, no one signed up. Almost a year would pass before Parke got his first assignment.

Still, the advertisement represented a development of considerable significance in the history of aviation: the first appearance of the professional test pilot. Here was a flier publicly offering to "take the risks," as Parke put it, "of testing experimental machines."

Since the earliest days of flight, most aircraft designers had served as their own test pilots. Otto Lilienthal, the German glider builder whose work led aviation's progress in the 1890s, had declared that only "systematic and energetic practice in actual flying experiments" could lead to "a quick development in human flight." He had backed up his words by making more than 2,000 flights, the last of which killed him. The Wright brothers too, of course, had been their own test pilots, although they were well aware of the dangers involved. "If you are looking for perfect safety," Wilbur Wright observed, "you will do well to sit on a fence and watch the birds, but if you really wish to learn you must mount a machine and become acquainted with its tricks by actual trial."

The Wrights and other designers in the first few years of aviation had little choice. There was no pool of experienced aviators around to do the flying for them, since the opportunity to learn to fly was largely restricted to those people who built their own airplanes. When Britain's Geoffrey de Havilland set out to design and construct a flying machine in 1908, he had never even seen a real airplane, much less flown one.

All of that was beginning to change at about the time Wilfred Parke advertised his services as a test pilot. A few manufacturers—the Wrights and Glenn Curtiss in America, Louis Blériot in France—had begun to produce aircraft for sale, and a number of flight schools

Featured on the cover of a Belgian sports magazine, the Deperdussin Monocoque Racer is heralded as "Victor of the Year" for its first-place finish in the 1912 Gordon Bennett race. The plane's streamlined fuselage, made possible by its revolutionary single-shell construction, enabled the French craft to set a speed record of 108.18 mph. The inset shows its namesake and manufacturer, Armand Deperdussin.

were turning out graduates who were eager to apply their skills.

Even more important, the science of aviation was starting to catch up with the development of aircraft. Designing a flying machine was becoming less an exercise of intuition and more a systematic application of known facts and well-founded theory. The process had begun to involve fewer lone pioneers and more teams of specialists, including the specialist who determined whether the aircraft was capable of performing as it was meant to: the test pilot.

These collaborative efforts spurred an astounding acceleration in the evolution of the airplane. In 1911, most aircraft were still frail biplane constructions of wood, fabric and piano wire much like the Wrights' first Flyer. The pilot sat in the open framework of struts and braces, trying to compel the aircraft to go where he wanted by means of a primitive control system, praying all the while that his erratic engine would keep the craft moving fast enough to hold it aloft.

Over succeeding years, innovation followed innovation, transforming the stick-and-wire contraption, feature by feature, into the basic form of the modern aircraft: a metal-skinned monoplane with a stream-lined fuselage, low cantilevered wings and sophisticated control surfaces that respond instantly to a pilot's command. As piston engines and propellers improved, power and speed increased to levels only dreamed of by the early designers, and then, with the advent of jet engines, to levels far beyond their dreams.

For the early test pilot, the smallest mistake—his own or the designer's or that of the lowliest mechanic—could, and often did, mean sudden death. This was particularly true when Wilfred Parke set himself up as a test pilot. In the first six months of 1911 there were 30 recorded fatal flying accidents in Europe and the United States, costing the lives of 34 pilots and passengers—this at a time when, for example, Britain's entire military air corps boasted a total of five airplanes and fewer than a dozen pilots. Such statistics did not deter Parke; it seemed that nothing could deter him when it came to flying. When his flight-school instructor first let him climb into an aircraft to try taxiing it, Parke immediately took off, flew a short distance, landed to turn the plane around (he was apparently prudent enough not to try an aerial turn without instruction) and then flew back. During his first year of flying he crashed twice—once into a sewage pond—but escaped injury both times. The "luck of Parke" became a byword among fellow pilots.

Parke at last found his wished-for opportunity to test new planes in the spring of 1912, when he teamed up with designer Alliott Verdon Roe, one of aviation's heroic pioneers. Several years earlier Roe had recognized the Wrights' achievement when others in Europe remained skeptical, and he resolved to build and fly an airplane himself. Working with almost no money, Roe had ridden a motorcycle each day to the Lea Marshes near London and there transferred the vehicle's nine-horsepower engine to a triplane that he was struggling to get into the air.

Pioneer test pilot Wilfred Parke emerges from the cabin of an Avro Type G biplane in 1912. Parke loved his hazardous calling, if for no other reason than the sheer joy of flying: "You feel like a king—it's so glorious!" he once exclaimed.

Billed as the "first totally enclosed aeroplane," the Avro Type F monoplane featured an aluminum cabin, primarily designed to streamline the fuselage rather than shelter the pilot. Indeed, many early designers feared that aviators might fall asleep without the icy wind in their faces.

At the end of a day's efforts he would remove the engine, reinstall it in the motorcycle and ride home. In 1909 the plane flew at last, and Roe's doggedness and brilliance had launched him on a career as one of Britain's leading designers and aircraft manufacturers.

When Parke began test-flying for him, Roe's fledgling firm Avro (for A. V. Roe) was building several planes for the British War Office, which had recently taken an interest in aviation. One machine Parke tested for Roe, a monoplane called the Avro Type F, was a landmark in aircraft design: It was the first plane with a completely enclosed cabin. What in retrospect seems a logical advance of considerable benefit to pilots was at the time widely regarded with suspicion by fliers, few of whom, said *Flight* magazine, "relished the idea of entering and operating an aeroplane as one would a submarine." Parke's test flights revealed that the Type F was too frail and underpowered to carry a reasonable payload. Roe abandoned it for a new design, the Type G, a biplane with a two-seat enclosed cabin. He finished the prototype in the summer of 1912, just in time for the first military airplane competition staged by the War Office. The Type G had never been in the air before Parke took off for a short flight at the start of the trials. The plane performed well in its initial outing, but a few days later Parke ran into trouble when he attempted to prove the Type G's endurance with a three-hour flight.

Cutting the flight short because of strong winds, Parke found himself compelled to make a downwind landing. Roe's cabin design had one great drawback: In the interest of reducing drag by smoothing the plane's contours, there was no window at the front. The pilot could look out small openings on either side, but had no way of seeing what lay directly ahead. Pushed from behind by the wind, the plane touched

Aerodynamics: why airplanes fly

At the end of the first decade of the 20th Century, aircraft designers knew more about building airplanes than about why they flew. But that gap was gradually being narrowed far from the flying fields by scientists who pursued a new discipline called aerodynamics, a branch of theoretical physics dealing with the behavior of air in motion.

Chief among the early aerodynamicists were two men, Ludwig Prandtl of Germany and Frederick W. Lanchester of Great Britain, who arrived independently at what would be known as the circulation theory of lift.

The two researchers drew on the work of earlier scientists, notably Switzerland's Daniel Bernoulli and Britain's Sir George Cayley. Bernoulli had found in 1738 that when the velocity of a fluid increases—and air is a fluid—its pressure decreases. Cayley had studied the lifting power of wings. After years of analysis Prandtl and Lanchester determined that lift results from nothing more than a difference in air pressure above and below a wing (*right, center*).

Prandtl also studied the nature of friction drag, one of three kinds of drag, or air resistance, that affect an airplane (*opposite*). He learned that the effects of friction drag were confined to the air closest to the wing surface—the boundary layer. Keeping the boundary layer flowing smoothly was essential to minimize friction drag.

Even as Prandtl was making these discoveries, Orville and Wilbur Wright had developed a theory of how propellers generate thrust, showing that each blade acts as a wing revolving vertically.

Such findings enabled designers to advance aviation beyond the intuitive stage and put the building and flying of planes on a firm scientific footing.

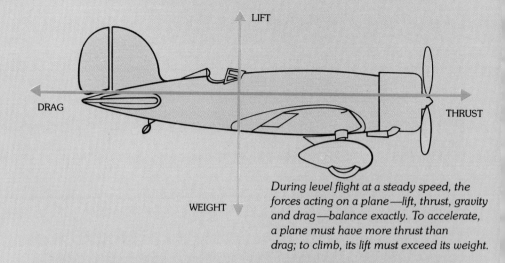

During level flight at a steady speed, the forces acting on a plane—lift, thrust, gravity and drag—balance exactly. To accelerate, a plane must have more thrust than drag; to climb, its lift must exceed its weight.

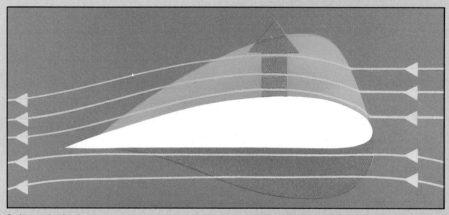

Lift results from air traveling faster over the curved top of a wing than beneath it. The difference in speed causes an area of low pressure above the wing that combines with an area of higher pressure below to lift the wing. The faster the airflow, the greater the lift.

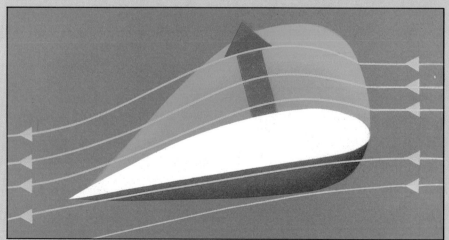

Lift can be increased by tilting the wing to a higher angle of attack, but only up to an angle of 15 degrees or so. Then the airflow becomes turbulent and destroys lift—the wing stalls.

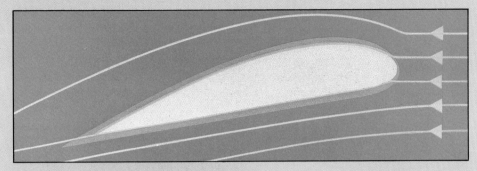

Friction drag is caused by the stickiness, or viscosity, of the air, which clings to the wings in what is called the boundary layer (green). Within this region, the air molecules touching the wing contribute more to drag than do the molecules at the edge of the boundary layer.

Form drag is a result of the air's resistance to a body that is passing through it. Blunt shapes create a great deal of form drag, particularly at high speeds. Thus the streamlining of aircraft, by reducing the number of components protruding into the airstream and by shaping the plane to smooth the flow of air past it, has assumed ever greater importance.

In this diagram, narrow bands of color show the parts of the airstream that cause induced drag. High-pressure flow below the wing (violet) curls around the wing tip into the low-pressure flow above it (blue), creating a spiral vortex that holds the plane back. Broad bands of color represent airflow far enough from the wing tip that it does not contribute to induced drag.

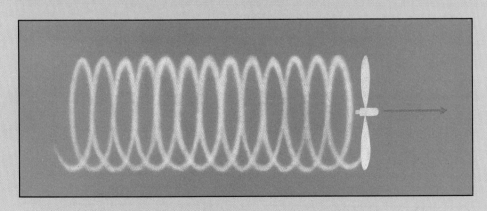

An airplane's propeller, which converts the engine's rotational energy into thrust, has blades that are actually airfoils. As they turn, the air passing across them creates a high-pressure area behind the propeller and a low-pressure area in front of it, thrusting the plane forward.

down and was barreling over the ground when a wheel struck a molehill that Parke could not see. The aircraft flipped tail over nose and slammed onto its back. It was almost completely demolished except for the cabin, in which Parke, unhurt, hung upside down by his safety belt.

The "luck of Parke" was challenged again in the flier's second attempt to pass the endurance test. This time the three hours passed without incident until Parke arrived back over the field for his landing. Eager to "finish with a bit of a flourish," he cut the throttle and banked the plane into what he intended to be a graceful spiral glide to earth. Then, believing his angle of descent to be too steep, he pulled back on the stick to lift the aircraft's nose.

But he lifted the nose too high; the airflow over the wings was abruptly interrupted, and the wings lost the lift that had kept the plane flying. In short, the aircraft stalled. Suddenly the nose dropped, and the plane began whirling toward the ground in a tight, dizzying spiral. Parke opened the throttle and pulled back on the stick, but the aircraft continued its relentless descent. He knew he was locked into what fliers then called a spiral dive (it later came to be known as a spin), a predicament few aviators had survived—and those who had could not explain how. He turned the rudder in the direction of the spin, like an automobile driver correcting for a skid, but the circular plunge continued. With just seconds to spare, Parke turned the rudder against the spin, and the plane immediately ceased its violent whirling, dropping into a straight dive. Parke then pulled back on the stick. "She flattened out," he said later, "and came under control at once."

Roe and fellow designer Geoffrey de Havilland had watched the drama from the field, certain that Parke was about to be killed. They raced to the plane after it landed, eager to learn how the pilot had recovered from the seemingly hopeless fix. Parke, who possessed the kind of keenly analytical mind that came to characterize good test pilots, was just as eager to describe what had happened, and related the story in detail. "Parke's dive," as it was known before the day was out, caused a sensation among fliers. His ruddering technique became part of the standard procedure for escaping from spins.

Unfortunately, Parke's luck and quick reflexes could not for long make up for the lack of one quality essential to a good test pilot: caution. Less than four months after surviving his famous dive, he broke two cardinal rules when flying a Handley Page monoplane at Hendon, north of London. He took off knowing the aircraft was having engine trouble, and then, when the engine failed in flight, he tried to turn back to the field without sufficient altitude or air speed. The plane stalled, and before Parke could recover from the ensuing spin, it slammed into the ground. Would-be rescuers had to saw apart the wreckage in order to remove Parke's body.

Parke left a legacy for aviation: a large notebook in which he had evaluated and analyzed in careful detail the flight characteristics of planes that he had flown. His reports—which he had collectively given

Pitch, yaw and roll

For stable flight, an airplane has to be kept from pitching up or down and also from yawing, or slewing from side to side. And the wings have to be kept level to prevent the craft from rolling. At the same time, a pilot must be able to make his plane climb or descend, turn or fly straight, by deliberately altering pitch, roll and yaw.

The Wright brothers, first to devise a practical aircraft control system, used elevators to regulate pitch, and mounted them at the nose of their biplane. Rudders at the tail controlled yaw. To govern roll, the Wrights invented wing warping, a means of twisting the airfoils to increase lift on one side of the plane and decrease it on the other.

As higher speeds made stiffer wings necessary, aircraft designers supplanted wing warping with ailerons. They also moved the elevators to the tail, near the rudder, for greater stability. And in time, they discovered that other arrangements were possible. High-speed jets, for example, commonly have no elevators at all. Pitch is controlled by a stabilator—a pivoting horizontal stabilizer—or if the aircraft has a delta wing, by elevons, control surfaces on the trailing edge of the wing, near the tail, that serve as both elevators and ailerons.

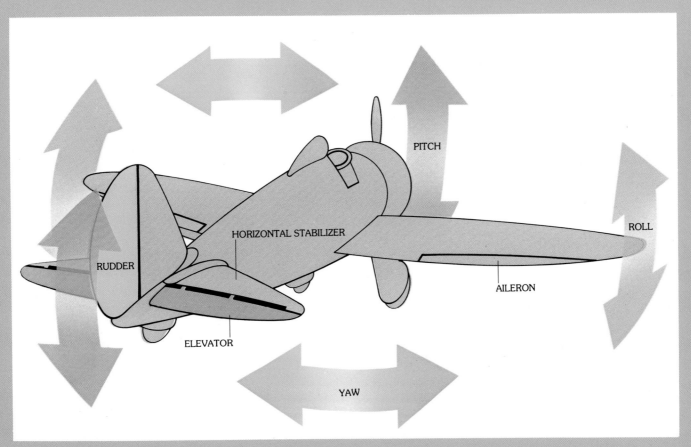

PITCH

ROLL

HORIZONTAL STABILIZER

RUDDER

AILERON

ELEVATOR

YAW

Aircraft control surfaces are color-coded in this diagram to represent the motion each imparts to a plane. Ailerons (yellow) produce roll, elevators (violet) alter pitch and the rudder (blue) makes the plane yaw.

the Latinate title *Aviaticanda*—were published in two British flying journals after his death and earned Parke wide recognition as a serious student and critic of aircraft performance.

Parke's work had been an important, if small, step toward the kind of methodical analysis that would underlie the development of the modern airplane. But at the time of his death in 1912, the precise physical nature of flight—why planes flew and, conversely, why they crashed—was still little understood. "Crashes were a normal feature of flying in that era," wrote Frank T. Courtney, a contemporary of Parke's who later became a leading test pilot. "Anything could cause a crash in days when engines were skittish, stability was a questionable curiosity, controls were erratic, structures were delicate, and piloting consisted largely of staggering along close to the stalling point. We tried to learn whatever we could from any crash, but most crashes remained unexplained. We just assumed that airplanes naturally crashed every so often."

But, as Courtney put it, "if we air people couldn't explain our crashes, that didn't deter the newspapers from doing so." On discovering that one pilot killed in an unexplained crash had been suffering from a head cold, a reporter deduced that the aviator might have lost control of the plane while sneezing. The newspaper followed up the journalist's story with editorial speculation about how many other crashes might have been caused by sneezes. "For a brief while," said Courtney, "the sneeze loomed as a major hazard of aviation." Obviously, the world still had a lot to learn about aircraft and flying.

In fact, the knowledge that would give designers and test pilots a clearer understanding of why their machines behaved as they did—knowledge that would enable aircraft design to advance beyond the perilous stick-and-wire stage—was steadily being acquired by men who did most of their work on the ground. By 1910, national aviation research centers, most of them government-funded, had been established in France, Germany, Great Britain and Russia. In 1915, the U.S. followed suit with the founding of the National Advisory Committee for Aeronautics (NACA); patterned on the European models, it would by the 1930s be the envy of Old World aeronautical experts.

The establishment of the national laboratories helped to bring order to an enterprise in which progress had been fitful. In the early years, most creators of new flying machines worked alone or with a single collaborator, and details of new discoveries were not freely disseminated. The same mistakes were repeated again and again by different inventors, and successful innovations were frequently ignored for years until they were rediscovered by later experimenters.

A case in point was the engine that American Charles Manly designed and built for Samuel Langley's ill-fated *Aerodrome,* a large tandem-winged craft that crumpled on takeoff and sank into the Potomac River two weeks before the Wright brothers first flew at Kitty Hawk. Manly's power plant was far superior to the Wrights'. A five-cylinder radial—

Englishman Geoffrey de Havilland—
pioneer designer and test pilot—assumes
a grave mien before taking off in his
B.E.3 in 1912. He went on to design the
D.H.4 reconnaissance bomber of
World War I fame, and to found his own
aircraft company after the War.

that is, its cylinders radiated out from the crankcase, like the spokes of a bicycle wheel—Manly's engine could produce 52.4 horsepower over a sustained period and weighed just 135 pounds, or 2.6 pounds per horsepower. The Wrights' in-line, four-cylinder engine turned out 12 horsepower and weighed 179 pounds—14.9 pounds per horsepower. But since Manly's engine was coupled to an airframe that failed ignominiously, its virtues were overlooked; more than a decade would pass before another aircraft engine matched its low weight-to-power ratio.

Such lags and hiccups in progress became less common when teams of specialists replaced lone designers as the prime movers behind aircraft evolution. Both the solitary and the collaborative approach marked the early work of the British designer Geoffrey de Havilland, whose career stretched from flight's pioneering days into the jet age.

Born the son of a poor English curate in 1882, de Havilland as a boy was fascinated with mechanical devices. After reading Jules Verne's novel *The Clipper of the Clouds,* he became captivated by the notion of powered flight. He attended an engineering school in London and spent a year as a draftsman for a motorcar company. Then, in 1908, his long-standing interest in flight hardened into resolution when Wilbur Wright demonstrated the Wright biplane in France. As he wrote later, "I read eagerly about Wright's astonishing displays, which were far ahead of anything achieved in Europe, and knew at once that this was the machine to which I was prepared to give my life."

He secured £1,000 from his grandfather, rented a workshop in London and hired a bright young mechanic, Frank Hearle, to assist him. Then de Havilland, who had never seen a flying machine, set out to create one. "I had managed to convince myself that there was no suitable engine available for the aeroplane," he later recalled, "partly because it was probably true anyway and partly because I was very keen to design my own.'' He drew up plans for a four-cylinder water-cooled engine of 50 horsepower, and while an automobile maker built it for him, he began designing the airframe. He read all he could find on the work of earlier designers before devising a biplane with a single engine mounted crosswise in the fuselage and driving two pusher propellers through beveled gears. ''Relatively few drawings were made,'' he said, ''and quite a bit of designing was done on the job.''

Using tools and materials purchased largely from hardware stores and lumberyards, de Havilland and Hearle started constructing the airplane. By November 1909 the project had outgrown the London workshop, so the men moved their operation to a pair of sheds on a country estate. There they assembled the aircraft and began a long series of ground tests that revealed one flaw after another.

Finally, after five months, de Havilland had enough confidence in the machine to try flying it. He taxied a short distance up a slope, turned the aircraft around so that it faced downhill into the wind, and began his takeoff run. ''I opened the throttle wider and wider. I was travelling faster than ever before down the hill, and I knew I was near the safety limit. This was the moment I was sure. I pulled back hard on the stick.''

The plane left the ground at so steep an angle that de Havilland found himself ''looking up into the clear sky, while my weight on the seat seemed suddenly to have increased alarmingly.'' Then he heard the crack of breaking wood as the overstressed structure broke up around him and crashed to the ground. Although stunned, de Havilland was not seriously hurt. Had the failure occurred at a higher altitude, he might well have perished, a fact not lost on the onlookers—including his father, who left the scene, said de Havilland, ''speechless with shock.''

Young de Havilland himself refused to ''waste any time on regrets.'' He immediately determined that the engine was salvageable and set to work constructing another aircraft, resolving that this time he ''would build an aeroplane that could fly.'' So he did. By installing the engine parallel to the fuselage and mounting a single pusher propeller directly on the engine shaft, he eliminated the earlier plane's heavy and problem-plagued system of gearboxes, drive shafts and twin propellers. He simplified the airframe, making it both lighter and stronger, and lightened the landing gear by using bicycle wheels. No. 2, as de Havilland called the plane, flew in the late summer of 1910. On the first flight the designer took it only inches off the ground, but he was soon maneuvering at an altitude of 100 feet. By autumn he was confident enough to take his wife and eight-week-old son Geoffrey up for a ride.

Soon after, de Havilland sold his flying machine for £400 to what was then His Majesty's Balloon Factory—soon to be called the Royal Aircraft Factory—at Farnborough. He signed on to work at the Factory as a designer and test pilot and brought Hearle along with him. Despite its name, the Factory was chiefly a research establishment that had concentrated on lighter-than-air craft. But a new official interest in airplanes was attracting talented scientists and engineers to Farnborough. These

Louie de Havilland, wife of the designer, pauses at her labors—stitching the heavy wing fabric for her husband's first plane.

men had expertise in such areas as aerodynamics, where de Havilland by his own admission was weak. Working with them, the young designer began to develop a number of successful aircraft.

But even at Farnborough, laboratory proofs and calculations often lagged behind test flights—sometimes with disastrous results. Such was the case with de Havilland's B.S.1, a small single-seat biplane conceived as a military scout. It eventually proved useful in that capacity, and came to be the acknowledged forerunner of the fighter plane, but only after a significant modification in the original design. When the prototype was built, the rudder appeared small in relation to the rest of the aircraft, but de Havilland did not believe this would cause any "serious trouble." During a test flight, however, he made a very tight turn, and the plane slipped into a violent spin. He applied full opposite rudder, but the control surface was too small to stop the spin. De Havilland survived the resulting crash, but suffered a broken jaw and lost many of his teeth—which a mechanic picked out of the wreckage and thoughtfully returned to the designer in an envelope. Recovering in the hospital, de Havilland was visited by an aerodynamics specialist from Farnborough. The designer wrote later that his visitor reported, "with a certain note of triumph, that they had made extensive calculations and the results proved that the rudder was too small."

"I tried," recalled de Havilland, who had already learned of the rudder's inadequacies the hard way, "to show interest."

One of de Havilland's colleagues at Farnborough was Edward "Teddy" Busk, a young Cambridge honors graduate who began his career at the Factory in 1912 as a nonflying assistant engineer but went on to become the world's first truly scientific test pilot. Busk's chief interest

De Havilland's earliest effort in airplane design awaits its 1909 maiden flight. Built of light wood, with two ungainly propellers, the craft rose only 20 feet before a wing tore away and the plane crashed to earth.

was in perfecting a design for a plane that would maintain stable flight without a pilot having constantly to adjust the controls.

He began his research with two de Havilland biplanes: the R.E.1 and the B.E.2, a two-seater that de Havilland himself had piloted to a British altitude record of 10,500 feet. Despite this achievement, the craft was decidedly unstable, which made it ideal for Busk's study. To find out just what happened to the airflow across the surfaces of the plane, Busk rigged tubes that would carry inrushing air from various points on the wings and tail to pressure gauges inside the cockpit. A pilot then had to take the plane, in calm air, through a precise pattern of climbs, dives and level runs, continually checking and noting his air speed and the pressure levels shown on the cockpit dials. The process had to be repeated again and again as the intake tubes were shifted about.

Unfortunately, the aviators who flew these tedious research missions did not fully understand Busk's experimental goals or the precision of measurement required. Busk was dismayed that the pilots sometimes did not mention, until long after the fact, events on their flights that would have drastically altered his interpretation of the data. After nine months of frustration he complained to his boss that it was impossible to get the information he needed unless he made the test flights himself. In the spring of 1913 he was given permission to take flying lessons from de Havilland and that summer began making his own research flights.

Busk translated his findings into changes that would make the B.E.2 more stable, and by May 1914 de Havilland and his small team at Farnborough had built a new version of the aircraft that incorporated the researcher's innovations. The wings were staggered (the lower wing was moved rearward of the upper one); ailerons replaced the crude wing warping that de Havilland had copied from the Wrights; the rudder had a fixed fin added in front of it, and the horizontal tail was entirely redesigned. The remodeling worked wonders; the modified craft, designated the B.E.2C, proved to be history's first truly stable airplane. Busk demonstrated its qualities in repeated flights during which he removed his hands and feet from the controls for as long as 10 minutes.

Just six months after the first flight of the modified aircraft, Busk was killed when the B.E.2C he was flying burst into flame, probably as a result of a spark from the engine igniting gasoline from the plane's chronically leaky fuel system. Yet in a test-flying career that lasted barely a year, his careful, deliberate approach had established a pattern for his successors. Partly because of Busk's example, the seat-of-the-pants daredevil test pilot was beginning to disappear in fact if not in fiction.

Aviation's early progress in France was not marked by the sort of organized collaboration that went on at Farnborough. Yet France was the most air-minded of nations before World War I, and news of innovation was more widely disseminated there than elsewhere, with the result that France's designers were comparatively quick to take advantage of one another's inspiration. The most impressive result of this process—the

British test pilot and engineer Edward "Teddy" Busk laughs gleefully after completing a stable flight in an R.E.1 biplane in 1913. Busk's innovations made the R.E.1 and the later B.E.2C capable of "hands off" flight. They could fly straight and level, adopt appropriate banking angles in turns and right themselves when gusts blew them out of proper orientation—all without the pilot having constantly to adjust the controls.

finest airplane of the prewar era—was the Deperdussin Monocoque Racer of 1912. The Racer's designer of record was a French engineer named Louis Béchereau, but it is fair to describe the aircraft as the cumulative creation of a number of aviation pioneers.

Among them were two French brothers, Louis and Laurent Seguin, owners of an automobile-engine company called Société des Moteurs Gnôme (the name was meant to evoke an image of small power plants busily at work.) In 1907 the Seguins decided to try their hands at aircraft engines. A common problem with existing engines was cooling. Planes moved so slowly that air-cooled engines did not get sufficient ventilation; they tended to heat up and lose power quickly. Water-cooled engines ran at lower temperatures when their cooling systems worked, but they were unreliable and generally heavier. Two years later, Laurent Seguin came up with a radical solution: an air-cooled rotary engine.

In a conventional aircraft engine, the pistons of fixed cylinders drove a revolving crankshaft that turned the propeller. In Seguin's rotary design, the crankshaft was stationary and the radially positioned cylinders revolved around it; the propeller was fixed to the engine block and rotated with the cylinders. Because Seguin's cylinders were continuously spinning through the air, they stayed cooler than stationary cylinders.

The brothers had to devise ingenious solutions to many problems inherent in the basic design—including a hollow crankshaft to feed a combustible mixture of air and fuel to the cylinders—but by 1909 they had turned out an engine that delivered 50 horsepower for a weight of only 165 pounds. Moreover, the Gnôme rotary ran much more smoothly than most existing engines, which sometimes vibrated so violently that they shook themselves loose from their frail airframes.

The Gnôme became the first successful mass-produced aircraft engine. It was sold by the hundreds, and later thousands, in versions with five, seven and nine cylinders. Soon Gnômes were being manufactured under license—and without license—in Germany, Britain and the U.S. And a Gnôme rotary was one of the elements that would make the Deperdussin Racer such a superb aircraft.

Not long after the Seguins developed their novel engine, a French-based Swiss boat builder named Eugene Ruchonnet turned his attention to aviation and came up with an equally radical and ingenious approach to building a fuselage. Ruchonnet never worked on the Deperdussin Racer, but he was primarily responsible for one of its most distinctive features: its monocoque, or single-shell, construction.

In 1910, the 33-year-old Ruchonnet obtained a French pilot's license and began to think about building a new kind of aircraft. He believed that an airplane's fuselage could be built up in layers like the hull of a boat, out of thin strips of wood glued together. Instead of being merely a covering for an internal framework of sticks and wires, the skin itself would carry the structural load of the airplane. A fuselage constructed by this method not only would be strong and rigid, but also could be extremely smooth and streamlined. He began work on a monoplane of

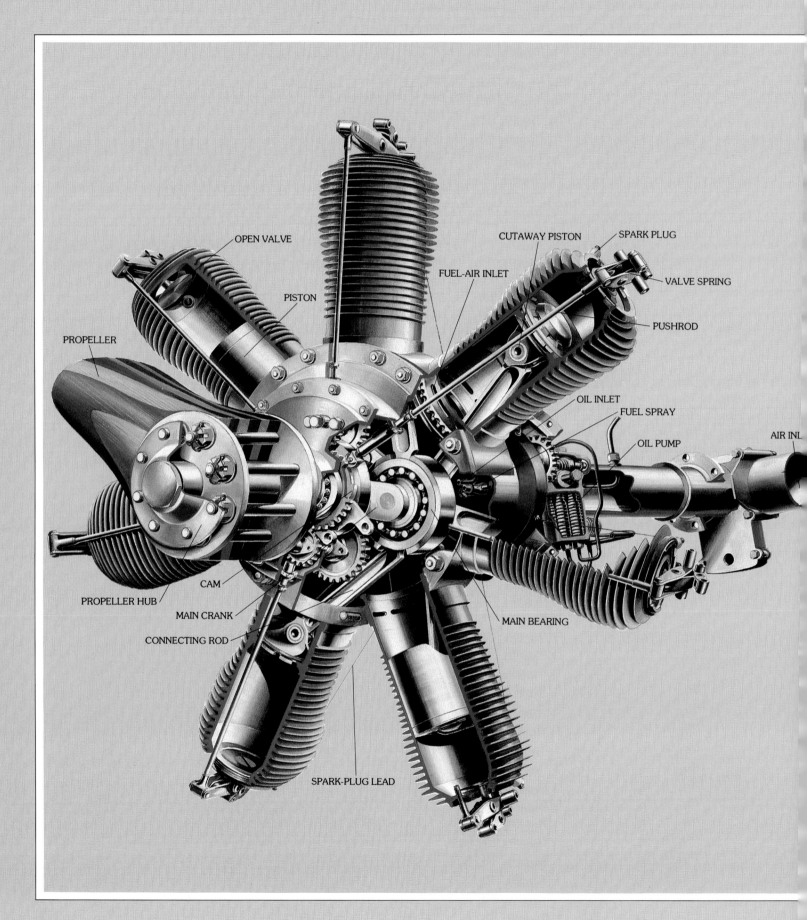

OPEN VALVE

CUTAWAY PISTON

SPARK PLUG

FUEL-AIR INLET

PISTON

VALVE SPRING

PROPELLER

PUSHROD

OIL INLET

FUEL SPRAY

OIL PUMP

AIR INL

CAM

PROPELLER HUB

MAIN CRANK

MAIN BEARING

CONNECTING ROD

SPARK-PLUG LEAD

An engine that spun to keep cool

The Gnôme rotary engine, designed in 1909 by two French brothers, Laurent and Louis Seguin, was one of early aviation's great breakthroughs. It was lighter than most contemporary water-cooled engines, with their failure-prone plumbing, and unlike other air-cooled engines of the day, it did not overheat.

The Gnôme cooled itself by spinning its cylinders through the air at 1,000 rpm. The engine revolved around a fixed crankshaft, thus turning the propeller, which was attached to the engine block. Early Gnômes generated 50 hp—far more than competing power plants— and their rotary action produced far less damaging vibration.

For all its power and reliability, the Gnôme had drawbacks. Because slowing down its rotation would inhibit cooling, it allowed no throttle changes; a pilot had to switch his engine off when he wanted to reduce speed. The revolving mass of the engine created strong torque that required special skills of the aviator. And the rotating cylinders sprayed out their lubricating fluid—castor oil—in a constant vapor that was blown back at the pilot. Aviators learned to their chagrin that continually breathing castor oil vapor had the same effect as swallowing a large dose for medicinal purposes.

This cutaway shows a seven-cylinder Gnôme with part of a propeller attached. Fuel and air enter the engine's central crankcase through the hollow crankshaft and pass into the cylinders through narrow inlets when the pistons are at the bottom of their downstroke. As the engine rotates, the central cam pushes each piston up, compressing the fuel-air mix. A spark plug then ignites it, and the explosion forces the piston down, driving further rotation.

monocoque construction in a hangar he rented at La Vidamée airdrome north of Paris. In a matter of months he produced a craft with a distinctive tapered wooden fuselage that earned it the nickname, ''the Ruchonnet Cigar.'' By early January 1912, he had flown the plane successfully, and it became a familiar sight in the sky over La Vidamée. Then, late on the afternoon of January 12, after completing several flights without incident, he took off for a short hop to the nearby community of St. Nicolas. Suddenly, from a height of about 300 feet, the aircraft slipped into a steep dive and crashed, killing Ruchonnet.

Louis Béchereau, a French engineer, had been following Ruchonnet's work. He recognized that the single-shell fuselage was a brilliant idea, whatever flaws the ''Cigar'' may have possessed. Two years before Ruchonnet's death, the 30-year-old Béchereau had joined forces with entrepreneur and aviation enthusiast Armand Deperdussin to create an aircraft-manufacturing firm. Béchereau's first design for the firm had been a trim monoplane with a conventional slab-sided fuselage that was rectangular in cross section. The plane was flown against better-known rival planes in a series of European air meets and official French government trials, and its excellent performance firmly established the Deperdussin company as a leader in the field. In late 1911, having recognized the merit of Ruchonnet's construction technique, Béchereau and his assistant, a young Dutch engineer named Frederick Koolhoven, determined to build a streamlined racer of monocoque construction, to be powered by the latest Gnôme engine.

Béchereau and Koolhoven conceived of a bullet-shaped fuselage with stubby monoplane wings and sharply sweptback tail surfaces. Nothing about the revolutionary craft was left unrefined. Its 14-cylinder, 140-horsepower Gnôme engine was enclosed in a smooth aluminum cowling; even its wooden landing-gear struts were streamlined.

But the most striking aspect of the Racer was the fuselage, which was circular in cross section and tapered almost to a point at the rear. It was created in two longitudinal halves using Ruchonnet's methods. Skilled woodworkers made a master form for each half. Over these they shaped a light framework of curved hickory supports, then fixed a layer of thin tulipwood strips to the hickory with pins and glue. Two more layers of tulipwood were added over the first, each forming a crosshatch pattern with the layer below to ensure rigidity. Next the workers removed the almost-completed sections from the forms, attached fabric to the inside of the shells to keep the wood from splitting, added the engine mounts and internal bracing for the pilot's seat and other equipment, and joined the halves together. Then they covered the entire fuselage with fabric, varnishing it for smoothness and added strength. The result was a single streamlined shell having maximum usable internal space, a beautiful aerodynamic form, exceptional rigidity and low weight.

The Racer's beauty was matched by its performance. Almost as soon as it was completed in January 1912, test pilot Jules Védrines flew it to a new world speed record of 90.02 miles per hour. The Racer set five more records over the next six months, winging past the milestone of 100 miles per hour in February and hitting 106.12 soon after. By the time the airplane arrived in Chicago for the Gordon Bennett race in September 1912, its reputation had scared off most challengers; the one plane American air-racing officials managed to press into the contest had mechanical trouble and failed to get off the ground. Undismayed by the lack of competition, Védrines raced around the course at a new record of 108.18 miles per hour. The next year, the Racer won the first Schneider Seaplane Trophy race and then a second Bennett race, exceeding 125 miles per hour in the process. Less than a decade after Kitty Hawk, the Deperdussin Monocoque Racer had quadrupled the speed of the Wrights' first Flyer, and for more than a decade to come its innovative features would influence aircraft design.

Early in flight's second decade, however, the attention of the aviation community was forcibly diverted from racers to another kind of aircraft: warplanes. When Europe erupted into battle in the summer of 1914, designers in all the belligerent nations rushed to respond to a new set of exigencies that had little to do with a plane's ability to best a rival over a closed-circuit speed course. Manufacturers had to keep up with reports from the front and incorporate the latest lessons of air fighting in their designs. No one was more successful in responding to these wartime needs than the "Flying Dutchman," Anthony Herman Gerard Fokker.

Fokker had left his native Holland for Germany in 1910, at the age of 20, to study auto mechanics, but ended up taking a course in flying and aircraft construction. Inside of a year, with money borrowed from his family and a few optimistic investors, he had built three monoplanes and was earning a reputation as a pilot and flying instructor. By the end of World War I, he ran one of Europe's foremost aircraft companies and had given his name to the most famous fighter planes in the world.

Though he did his best to claim credit for designing these planes, Fokker, by the time the War started, was no longer a designer; rather, he was a canny entrepreneur alert to all the latest developments in his industry and to the needs of the German Air Service. Moreover, he was a superb test pilot; he always insisted on being the first to fly his company's new models, and he possessed an extraordinary intuitive ability to assess the qualities of an aircraft and suggest useful modifications.

Fokker may have been reluctant to acknowledge it to others, but he appears to have been aware of his own limitations as a designer, in so far as he regularly managed to find collaborators more technically competent than he himself was. On his earliest warplanes, he worked closely with a young German engineer named Martin Kreutzer. Together they were largely responsible for the light, maneuverable Fokker *Eindecker* (monoplane), which reached the Western Front in the summer of 1915. The plane was equipped with a synchronizing mechanism devised by Fokker and two other engineers that permitted a machine gun to be fired forward between the spinning blades of the plane's propeller. The fighter was so effective against the comparatively clumsy and under-

Frenchman Jules Védrines appears as the conqueror of the Pyrenees in this 1911 illustration commemorating his flight from Paris to Madrid in a Morane-Saulnier monoplane. The aviator claimed that during the trip he was attacked by an enraged mountain eagle at an altitude of more than 7,000 feet.

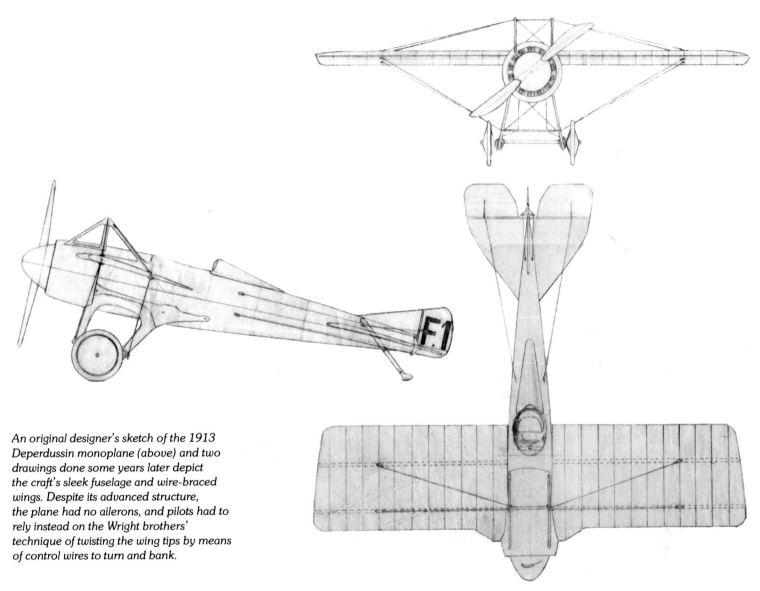

An original designer's sketch of the 1913 Deperdussin monoplane (above) and two drawings done some years later depict the craft's sleek fuselage and wire-braced wings. Despite its advanced structure, the plane had no ailerons, and pilots had to rely instead on the Wright brothers' technique of twisting the wing tips by means of control wires to turn and bank.

armed Allied aircraft that the British press decried what it called the "Fokker scourge," and the products of the Royal Aircraft Factory at Farnborough were spoken of in Parliament as "Fokker fodder."

After Martin Kreutzer's death during a test flight in June 1916, Fokker turned to Reinhold Platz for his company's designs. Platz had joined the firm as a welder in 1912, after spending eight years perfecting and demonstrating the then-new technique of acetylene welding to engineers in Germany, Switzerland and Russia. So proficient had he become that the welded-steel-tube fuselage frameworks he produced for Fokker persuaded German authorities to relax the ban placed on the use of such frames because of their previous structural failures.

Kreutzer's death gave Platz the opportunity to apply his intuitive engineering skills to the design of an entire aircraft. The first he developed was so radical a departure from conventional planes of the day that the military authorities refused to buy it, despite evidence of its superior performance. The craft was a small biplane with exceptionally

clean lines. Fokker called it the V.1, V standing for *verspannungslos* (without braces). The initial referred to the plane's outstanding feature—its thick, cantilevered wings. There were no drag-producing struts or wires to support the wings—they were internally braced with sturdy spars of pine-and-birch plywood running the length of their span. But the very absence of external supports worried the military procurement officers. Fokker, in his autobiography, described their initial reaction to the plane. "They were struck by a chilling silence," he wrote. "Staring coldly at my biplane, they walked around it as if it would bite. Someone wondered idiotically what was going to keep the wings on. They felt the wings as if doubting they were real; wiggled them tentatively as if expecting them to drop off. By a common instinct they began to shake their heads with comic dubiety like a Gilbert and Sullivan chorus of judges. They wanted something visible supporting the wings."

Desperately, Fokker demonstrated the biplane, flying it "as it had never been flown before, submitting it to every stress and strain of combat flying." But, wrote Fokker, the officers' "minds had crystallized in opposition. They seemed a little disappointed that the wings hadn't fallen off in the air to support their views."

A few months later, Platz designed a triplane with cantilevered wings

Dutch plane maker Anthony Fokker sits at the controls of his first aircraft, built in 1910. Like most pioneer aviators, he taught himself to fly through trial and error: "What astounded me," he later wrote, "was the variety of ways an aircraft could try to kill its pilot."

in response to the air command's call for a fighter to stand up against the British Sopwith triplane. After the military reaction to the V.1, however, Fokker and Platz prudently added a pair of streamlined struts connecting the three wings at their tips. (As it happened, the struts proved useful in controlling wing flutter.) The Air Service bought the exceptionally agile little triplane, which under the designation Dr.I *(Dr.* for *Dreidecker),* became the chosen aircraft of such German aces as Werner Voss and the entire Flying Circus of Baron Manfred von Richthofen.

Platz's next production plane, the D.VII, was acknowledged the finest mass-produced fighter of the War. It was another thick-winged, essentially cantilevered biplane, but like the Dr.I, it had a pair of struts linking the wing tips ("in deference to conservatism," Fokker later explained). The D.VII was fast, sturdy, maneuverable and extraordinarily easy to fly, but its chief virtue—a result of Platz's thick airfoil—was its ability to climb. A gentle tug on the stick and a push on the throttle, and the Fokker would shoot seemingly straight up. It could easily get on top of anything else in the sky, and it took a fearful toll of Allied aircraft once it became the standard frontline fighter in the summer of 1918.

An indication of the D.VII's effectiveness was the length to which German fighter pilots would go to be assigned the planes. Other German aircraft manufacturers had used their political influence—exploiting, in particular, the fact of Fokker's foreign nationality—to make certain that their own planes got the best Mercedes and BMW power plants available. Fokker's D.VII's were at first allocated less reliable and powerful engines. Consequently, said Fokker, some of the fliers assigned to other aircraft "deliberately cracked them up in order to salvage the engine to install in a Fokker D.VII." It should be noted, however, that Fokker was said to have offered bounties of sybaritic weekends in Berlin to pilots who produced such prized salvage for his machines.

The Fokker V.1 biplane fighter, built in 1916, shows its strutless design. German military authorities rejected the plane because its internally braced wings appeared too frail for combat. Fokker later insisted the decision resulted from a political intrigue abetted by rival aircraft manufacturers.

Though Platz's airplanes probably did more than those of any other designer to advertise the lifting power and aerodynamic efficiency of the thick, cantilevered (or semicantilevered) wing, the design did not originate with him. In 1911, at the French military air show, French designer Léon Levavasseur introduced an elegant, streamlined craft he called the *Monobloc Antoinette*. It was a three-seat monoplane with a fully enclosed fuselage, an undercarriage encased in aerodynamic ''spats'' and thick, cantilevered wings. Unfortunately, the wings and streamlining features were so heavy that no engine of the period was able to get the *Monobloc* off the ground for more than a few yards. But pictures of it were published around the world, and they may have made an impression on Platz and Fokker.

The man Fokker himself credits as the father of the thick-winged airplane was a German professor of thermodynamics named Hugo Junkers. In 1910, Junkers patented a design for a flying wing, and though the radical craft was never built, the patent is the first recorded design of a thick, self-supporting wing. Five years later, Junkers incorporated the same principles in his design for one of history's most signifi-

At the Junkers plant in Dessau, Germany, five factory employees stand on an experimental all-metal wing in 1915 to demonstrate its superior strength. The wing's internally braced structure enabled it to support the plane's weight without the need for drag-producing wires and struts.

cant airplanes. This was the J.1, which not only featured the first practical cantilevered wing, but was also the first all-metal aircraft.

Junkers, in addition to his academic duties, was a manufacturer of metal hot-water heaters. The Wrights' European tours of 1908 and 1909 aroused his interest in flight, and he began to devise a means of building an airplane with durable sheet metal, applying the knowledge he had gained making water heaters. The result was the J.1, a small monoplane built entirely of iron and steel and intended as a scout. Powered by a 120-horsepower Mercedes engine, it first flew in December 1915, reaching a speed of 105 miles per hour—quite creditable for the time. But it climbed slowly and moved ponderously compared with the nimble fabric-covered biplanes of the day, and it won no favor with pilots or the German military authorities, who refused to buy it.

Junkers, however, persevered with his radical designs, benefiting from the development of more powerful engines and a strong, lightweight aluminum alloy called duralumin. In 1917, the German Air Service bought his J.4, a two-seat biplane with semicantilevered wings. It was powered by a 200-horsepower engine and built largely of duralumin, which was corrugated for added strength, the corrugations running streamwise—from nose to tail—to minimize drag. Sheet-steel armor protected the cockpits, engine and fuel tank, since the J.4 was to be a ground-attack plane, or "trench strafer," and would be subjected to heavy small-arms fire. With all its metal the J.4 was anything but agile, but German airmen liked it for the protection it afforded them, and Allied fliers found it almost impossible to shoot down.

Junkers turned out two more significant warplanes before the end of the conflict, the J.9 and J.10. Both were all-metal cantilevered monoplanes like the J.1, but their wings were attached to the bottom rather than the middle or top of the fuselage as on all previous monoplanes. Conventional wisdom held that low wings would put a plane's center of gravity so high as to make it dangerously unstable, but the two Junkers planes proved perfectly stable. Their low wing position offered additional protection to the crew in the event of a crash, since the wings would hit the ground first and absorb some of the impact. Low wings were later found to provide a significant benefit in aircraft employing retractable landing gear: The undercarriage could be folded into the wings, and since the wings were low, the gear could be short and therefore light.

By the end of World War I, Junkers had thus contributed two key features to what, over the next 15 years, would become the standard modern aircraft—low, cantilevered monoplane wings and all-metal construction. These features had still to be refined through the use of monocoque or stressed-skin design, and great strides were to be made in streamlining and propulsion. But it was clear by 1919 that the era of stick-and-wire airframes and borrowed motorcycle engines was well and truly ended, as was the day of the seat-of-the-pants test pilot and the backyard designer. And yet aviation still needed adventurous geniuses, and there were many eager to assume the role. ～

2

In pursuit of speed and reliability

Late in the afternoon of June 14, 1922, a small monoplane touched down at a new airfield just outside Monmouth, Illinois. Arrayed on the erstwhile pasture were nearly 30 other aircraft, most of them conventional biplanes, gathered for a competition called the Midwestern Flying Meet, due to start the next day. The assembled pilots and enthusiasts had seen single-winged aircraft before, but this one caused a minor sensation. In front of its conventional open cockpit, the plane had seats for four passengers in an enclosed cabin—a feature almost unknown in American aircraft of the era. And the wing, mounted on top of the cabin, was braced by two distinctive struts extending from the bottom of the fuselage upward and outward to the underside of the wing. These were not the usual wooden or metal rods; they were fabric-covered airfoils that looked like slanted wings.

For all the attention the unusual plane attracted, not much could have been expected of it in the coming meet. It had first been flown only seven days before, and it was up against such competition-proven craft as the rugged Laird Swallow and the elegant Curtiss Oriole. Yet the monoplane—with a reconditioned 90-horsepower Anzani radial engine—won every event it entered. It outraced the Oriole by better than two minutes over a 15-mile course, even though the Oriole's engine was nearly twice as powerful. It outclimbed all competing aircraft by more than 1,000 feet in a 15-minute timed ascent, and it outglided them in a test that required pilots to cut their engines at 2,000 feet and then remain aloft as long as possible. The monoplane stayed up four minutes and 43 seconds, a full minute longer than its nearest competitor.

At the close of the meet, four trophies went to the monoplane's designer, a 36-year-old Sicilian immigrant named Giuseppe Bellanca. His triumphant new aircraft, which he called the Bellanca CF—C for commercial, F to denote his sixth design—had earned a prize for each of its victories and one for best plane overall. The trophies were the first public recognition given the man who would create some of the finest aircraft of the 1920s, planes that spanned oceans and continents and helped to show that flying machines were practical vehicles.

In less than 20 years following World War I, the work of geniuses such

Shortly after landing his H-1 racer at Newark Airport in 1937, Howard Hughes answers questions about his record-setting 7 hour 28 minute cross-country flight from Burbank, California.

as Bellanca and Jack Northrop, together with the stimulus of a few visionary eccentrics such as Howard Hughes, would make the U.S. the world leader in aircraft development. These designers, supported by such progressive companies as Lockheed, Boeing and Douglas, would transform civil aviation by the late 1930s. The widely acclaimed achievements of their pioneering craft would help to convince a skeptical public that airplanes were more than just weapons, or toys for rich daredevils—that they were a fast, reliable means of transportation.

Giuseppe Bellanca, like other brilliant airplane designers, seems almost to have been born to aviation. As a boy, he was fascinated by the flight of shore birds in his native Sicily. While studying mathematics and engineering at a technical college in Milan, he and two fellow students created the first aircraft designed and built in Italy to leave the ground under its own power. A pusher biplane, it flew just once, briefly, in 1909.

After Bellanca immigrated to the United States in 1911, he set to work building another airplane in the back room of his brother's Brooklyn grocery store. With that machine, a parasol monoplane, he first taught himself to fly and then trained others—among them the future World War I bomber pilot and mayor of New York City, Fiorello La Guardia. During the War, Bellanca designed two biplane trainers for a small firm in Maryland. The company failed after the War, but the trainers earned Bellanca something of a reputation in aviation circles. In 1921 a group of Omaha investors approached him. They wanted to produce an innovative aircraft for what they hoped would be a boom in commercial aviation, and they asked him to create the plane. Bellanca, who was already at work on his design for the CF, accepted. Though the firm folded a few months later, he found partners in Omaha to supply additional backing and completed work on the CF early in June of 1922.

In the weeks following its auspicious debut at the Midwestern Flying Meet, the monoplane collected nine additional trophies at two more flying competitions, again winning every event in which it was entered. The pilots who flew it—veteran Air Mail fliers Harry Smith and William Hopson—were dazzled with the monoplane's performance. "The plane has a rare combination of stability and maneuverability," wrote Smith. "I flew it six or eight complete circles in a bank of about 30 degrees with hands off the stick, controlling the plane entirely with the rudder. With the throttle at cruising position, the plane will fly hands-off without gaining or losing altitude. Open the throttle a little and the plane will slightly nose up and begin to climb. Close the throttle entirely and the plane will take a good normal gliding position. It goes into a spin with some difficulty and comes out extremely easy."

Hopson, who succeeded Smith as the CF's pilot after the first flying competition, placed little credence in such glowing reports. "When I went out to take my initial hop in the Bellanca," he wrote, "I went up a skeptic but came down a firm believer. For climb, speed, gliding, weight carrying and ease of operation under all conditions of practical flying, she is years ahead of any plane in the world today."

The accolades were not altogether spontaneous. One of Bellanca's partners, an Omaha motorcycle dealer named Victor Roos, had asked both pilots to write letters detailing their impressions of the CF. Roos wanted to use the testimonials to drum up orders for the $5,000 plane. Nonetheless, the praise was well deserved. The CF not only handled superbly, it was also exceptionally efficient. It could lift more than its own weight in fuel and cargo, and while cruising fully loaded at nearly 100 miles per hour, it consumed fuel at half the rate of comparable planes.

The CF had several features that contributed to its remarkable efficiency. Most obvious were the airfoil struts, which not only looked but functioned like additional wings, contributing significantly to the plane's overall lift. The fuselage had the profile of a giant airfoil, so that it, too, added lift. The wing had contours that presaged the highly refined, low-drag airfoils of a much later generation, and the generally clean lines of the plane minimized form drag. But even when all of these points were taken together, they did not account for the plane's remarkable performance, which analysts have only been able to ascribe to the unique "touch" of the designer. But neither Bellanca's touch nor Roos's energetic promotion could persuade buyers to purchase the CF, when for

Seated in the cockpit of his partially assembled Model J, self-taught pilot and design pioneer Giuseppe Bellanca confers with his backer, A. R. Martine. Built in 1927, the Model J was almost identical to the designer's previous plane, the W.B.2. But it contained an extra-large fuel tank—partially visible behind Bellanca—that enabled the craft to stay aloft for a record 51 hours 52 minutes on January 13, 1928.

the same price they could pick up a whole fleet of war-surplus Jennies.

While waiting in vain to sell even one CF, Bellanca earned a living by modifying a few Air Mail Service biplanes, substituting wings of his own design and adding pairs of lifting struts. Then, in March of 1925, he was offered another opportunity to design a plane from scratch. It came from the Wright Aeronautical Corporation of New Jersey, builders of the Whirlwind radial engine. The Whirlwind was both more dependable and more fuel-efficient than any previous air-cooled engine, and its manufacturers were looking for a plane to show it off. Wright's test pilot, Clarence Chamberlin, had barnstormed in one of Bellanca's biplane trainers and had formed an excellent opinion of the aircraft and its designer. He recommended Bellanca to his employers, and they commissioned the designer to create the ideal aircraft for their engine.

Bellanca worked through the spring developing the new design—a six-seat cabin monoplane, with room for the pilot to sit inside. He further refined his high-lift airfoil from the CF and took the new shape to New York University's wind tunnel for testing. Jerome Lederer, then in charge of the tunnel, remembered encountering Bellanca at the university. "A small, dark man dressed in shabby clothes came up to me. He was carrying something wrapped in newspaper. He asked me a question and I didn't understand what he said. I supposed he was looking for a laborer's job so I directed him to the employment office. Later that day I was working for him, testing that remarkable airfoil."

Evidently satisfied with the results of the tests, Bellanca and a crew at the Wright plant began construction of the first of the celebrated Wright-Bellancas. The W.B.1 was completed in September, and like the CF, it soon began taking prizes in flying competitions. In one instance, the efficiency contest at the 1925 National Air Races on Long Island, it scored half again as many points as the second-place finisher.

Early in 1926, the W.B.1 crashed during tests to determine its maximum load. The company quickly built a successor—the W.B.2—a slightly modified version of the original fitted with a more advanced Whirlwind, the J-5. Even compared with its noted predecessor, the new Whirlwind was a marvel of dependability—widely acknowledged the first truly reliable aircraft engine ever built. And perhaps more important, it was exceptionally sparing of fuel, thanks to a revolutionary valve designed by Samuel Heron, an Englishman working for the U.S. Army at Wright Field in Ohio. The stem of the new valve was filled with liquid sodium, a superb conductor of heat. The sodium transferred heat quickly from the head of the valve inside the cylinders to the stem, where it was dissipated. This allowed the engine to be fed a lean, economical fuel-air mixture, which burned at a much higher temperature than the rich, wasteful mixtures required by earlier air-cooled engines.

The W.B.2, like the W.B.1, ran up an impressive string of competitive victories. Wright had initially considered mass-producing the aircraft, but decided late in 1926 to sell off the W.B.2 and confine itself to making engines. Charles Lindbergh, in whom the plane had sparked

High-lift airfoils for low-speed flight

Flying an airplane at low speed or forcing it to climb too steeply can be perilous; there is the danger that the plane will stall and crash.

Gustav V. Lachmann, a German pilot, was first to propose a device to alleviate this hazard. His idea was a brilliant one: to build one or more slats, separated by slots, into the leading edge of a wing (below, top). At high speeds, with the wing at a low angle of attack, the airflow would bypass the slots; consequently, the slats would have no effect. But at low speeds, when a pilot angled a wing upward to get the most lift possible, air would flow through the slots and turn the slats into airfoils for added lift.

Later, Lachmann and British aircraft builder Frederick Handley Page, inventor of a similar device, collaborated on a slat that a pilot could extend at will.

By then, American engineer Harlan Fowler had designed a high-lift device for a wing's trailing edge—a flap that delivered a 90 per cent boost in lift. Used together, slats and flaps greatly shortened takeoff runs, lowered landing speeds and increased rates of climb.

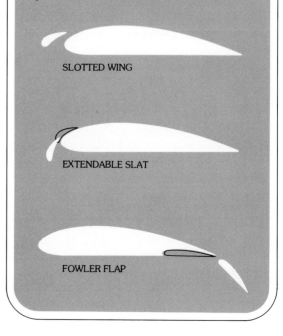

SLOTTED WING

EXTENDABLE SLAT

FOWLER FLAP

the idea of flying the Atlantic Ocean, offered $25,000 for the W.B.2. But the company turned him down, fearing adverse publicity for its engines should the seemingly rash young pilot be lost at sea.

Early in 1927, Wright closed a deal with New York millionaire Charles Levine, selling the W.B.2 and production rights for the design to Levine's newly created Columbia Aircraft Corporation. Bellanca was to be its president. Lindbergh ultimately commissioned Ryan Airlines in California to build the *Spirit of St. Louis* for his epochal flight to Paris on May 20. The W.B.2, meanwhile, was grounded in a brief legal dispute between Levine and a pilot he had fired.

On June 4, Levine and Clarence Chamberlin took off from New York in the W.B.2, renamed *Columbia,* bound for Berlin in an effort to best Lindbergh. They reached Germany, but became lost in bad weather and, running low on fuel, were forced to land in a wheat field, short of their goal. The *Columbia* had been aloft for 43 hours, 10 hours longer than the *Spirit of St. Louis,* and it had traveled 295 miles farther, but it had not reached Berlin and it had not been first across the Atlantic.

By this time, however, Bellanca had had enough of the mercurial Levine and had severed ties with his company. Still, the designer received a measure of recognition for the Chamberlin-Levine flight, and after his picture appeared on the cover of *Time* in July 1927, he was asked by the du Pont family to set up an aircraft manufacturing firm in Delaware. There he continued to build remarkably efficient single-engined monoplanes of the same basic configuration as the W.B.2. Like their predecessors, these aircraft set record after record. One, powered by a diesel engine, stayed aloft without refueling for 84 hours 33 minutes; another flew nonstop from New York to Istanbul, a distance of more than 5,000 miles; yet another was the first plane to span the Pacific, flying nonstop from northern Japan to Wenatchee, Washington.

Bellanca did nothing to discourage such record breaking, but none of his aircraft was ever built, as the *Spirit of St. Louis* was, exclusively for a spectacular long-distance flight. "We are making airplanes today," he wrote in 1928, "not for dramatic adventure but to meet the swiftly rising demand for dependable means of air transport. From my earliest experiments 22 years ago, I have not deviated from my original objective, which was to design and build an airplane to unite maximum safety and the greatest possible efficiency, as measured by speed, load and range."

In that, Bellanca succeeded admirably. Hundreds of his braced-wing monoplanes were used for decades all over the world as light transports and private passenger craft. But partly because he adhered to the basic design he had pioneered with the CF, his later planes were never at the forefront of aviation's rapid advance in the late '20s and early '30s, and Bellanca never received the acclaim his brilliant early creations merited.

On the Fourth of July, 1927, a month to the day after the *Columbia* took off for Germany, an elegantly streamlined new aircraft made its maiden flight from a hayfield that would later be a corner of Los Angeles International Airport. The plane was the prototype of the Lockheed Vega, the first aircraft to incorporate both a monocoque fuselage and a fully cantilevered wing. The Vega was also the first of a series of innovative single-engined monoplanes to emerge over the next five years from the struggling Lockheed Aircraft Company.

The Vega introduced a new generation of streamlined aircraft that would soon eclipse planes like the W.B.2. Yet in a surprising number of features, the two craft were closely comparable. Both were high-wing cabin monoplanes; both used a single Whirlwind J-5 engine; both had approximately the same weight, the same wing area and the same fuselage length. But where Bellanca's plane was designed for load-carrying efficiency, the Vega was built for speed. Its monocoque fuselage radically reduced drag by presenting about 35 per cent less frontal area to the wind. And its cantilevered wing—with no airfoil struts like the Bellanca's—had a span five feet shorter, a design that cut down on both drag and lift. The result was that while the Vega could carry less weight than the Bellanca, it could fly faster.

The difference in speed may have seemed insignificant at first—10 miles per hour in 1927—but with the arrival of more powerful engines, the advantages of the Vega's streamlined shape became apparent. By 1930, the Vega's top speed would approach 200 miles per hour. And from the outset, its monocoque, cantilevered construction was clearly a significant advance—a radical departure from the traditional slab-sided body and externally braced wing that Bellanca had refined to the limit of their potential. The Vega pointed the way to aviation's future.

This enormously influential little aircraft was the product of a firm that had just recovered from bankruptcy and would fail again before emerging in the late 1930s as one of the giants of the industry. The business had been founded in 1912 as the Alco Hydro-Aeroplane Company by the brothers Allan and Malcolm Loughead of San Francisco. The two were helped indirectly by their older brother Victor, who some years earlier had left California, where all of them were raised, and had established himself in Chicago as an automotive engineer. On the side, Victor was an aeronautical theorist with several books to his credit.

Through Victor, 21-year-old Allan had landed a job in Chicago in 1910 as one of the area's few airplane mechanics. He learned to fly, picked up the rudiments of aircraft design and in 1911 returned to San Francisco to collaborate with Malcolm, an auto mechanic, in building an airplane of their own. With money borrowed from a local taxicab operator, they constructed a two-seat flying boat; in time, they made enough money ferrying passengers around the Bay area to start a new venture, the Loughead Aircraft Manufacturing Company, in Santa Barbara.

There, early in 1916, the brothers attracted backing from a machine-shop owner and began work on a 10-passenger flying boat. News of the project reached 20-year-old John K. Northrop, an architectural drafts-man and part-time auto mechanic who was fascinated with planes. One morning in the summer of 1916, he turned up at the Loughead shop

A billboard at Santa Barbara proclaims the size and safety of the new Loughead— later spelled Lockheed—"Twin-motored ten passenger seaplane." The F-1, as this flying boat was designated, set a record in 1918 by remaining aloft for 181 minutes, on a flight from Santa Barbara to San Diego.

and asked for a job. The brothers put him to work on the hull of the flying boat, and before long he was designing the 74-foot upper wing of what was to be the world's largest seaplane. The F-1, as it was called, first flew in March 1918 and soon won the firm a Navy contract to build two more flying boats to the specifications of an existing Curtiss design.

At War's end, the Loughead brothers turned their attention to a civilian craft they called the S-1. It was to be a small, inexpensive single-seat biplane that they hoped might become the Model T of the aircraft industry. Its power plant, designed by the Loughead brothers and factory manager Tony Stadlman, was a two-cylinder, water-cooled engine that delivered 25 horsepower and ran for an hour on a gallon of gasoline. The wings folded back along the fuselage so that the plane could be stored in an ordinary garage, and it featured a novel speed brake devised by Northrop for landing on short runways. Northrop got the idea from sea gulls. He and some workmen scattered dead fish in a vacant lot near the waterfront. There Northrop noted that the gulls curled the trailing edges of their wings downward, into the airstream, as they landed to pick up the fish. Following this example of aerodynamic braking, he devised an ingenious system of struts and wires that enabled him to pivot the biplane's entire lower wing to a position almost perpendicular to the airflow during landings. But as it turned out, the device would seldom be needed; the S-1 was so light—800 pounds fully loaded—and buoyant that it could land at a mere 25 miles per hour.

The S-1's most significant feature was its monocoque fuselage, a design pioneered before World War I in the Deperdussin Racer and the Ruchonnet Cigar. But unlike those earlier monocoques, each of which

In 1918 officials of the fledgling Loughead Aircraft Manufacturing Company gather around one of the two modified Curtiss HS2L seaplanes the company built for the U.S. Navy. Malcolm Loughead is standing in the gun turret; his younger brother, Allan, is second from right. At Allan's left is apprentice Jack Northrop, who later founded his own aircraft company.

Shaping skins of wood in a concrete mold

From the first Vega in 1927 to the last Orion in 1934, Lockheed's celebrated line of single-engined wooden monoplanes shared the same monocoque fuselage. And each was made the same way, one side at a time, using a method devised in 1918 for the company's unsuccessful sport biplane, the S-1.

The technique called for a concrete mold that looked like a 27-foot bathtub. The mold was first lined with a set of thin, precisely cut strips of spruce arranged lengthwise and coated with glue. Then a second set of strips, temporarily fastened to a frame that bent them into a semicircular shape, was laid into the mold crosswise over the first set and coated with glue. After the frame was removed, a third set of strips was placed lengthwise on top of the second. Aligning and gluing the three layers of the shell, once a laborious procedure that required scores of man-hours, took about 20 minutes with the ingenious Lockheed process.

Next, a lid with an inflatable rubber bag inside was secured over the mold. Pumped up to high pressure, the bag forced the strips tight against the sides of the mold. A day later, workmen would remove a fully formed half of a fuselage shell—strong and rigid, yet less than a quarter inch thick.

Lockheed workmen lower the second layer of spruce strips, bent on their frame, into the concrete fuselage mold; the mold's lid, with its inflatable rubber bag, is suspended above. To make the fuselage of a Vega (left) or one of its sister "plywood bullets," two half shells were fastened with barbed nails and glue to a frame of wooden hoops and stringers (inset). Then they were sanded, covered with muslin and lacquered.

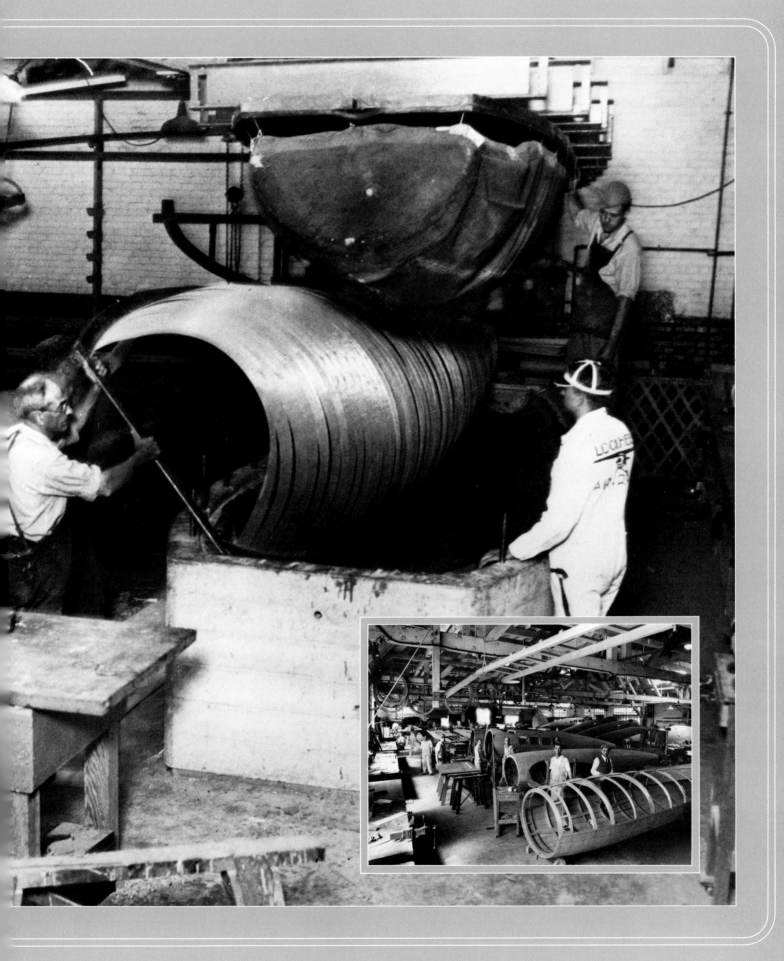

required scores of painstaking man-hours to shape, pin and glue its wooden shell, the S-1 fuselage was formed in a simple mold using a fraction of the labor expended on its predecessors *(pages 46-47)*.

The S-1 prototype was completed in 1920, but like Bellanca's CF, it was unable, despite its obvious merits, to attract buyers in the hopelessly glutted postwar aviation market. The Loughead Company had invested nearly $30,000 in the project and the failure was devastating; in 1921, Loughead Aircraft closed its doors and its assets were liquidated. For the next five years it would exist only in Allan Loughead's imagination. Jack Northrop joined Douglas Aircraft in Santa Monica. Malcolm Loughead moved to Detroit to develop an automobile hydraulic-brake system that he had invented some years earlier. Weary of hearing his name pronounced "loghead," Malcolm called his enterprise the Lockheed Hydraulic Brake Company. It soon succeeded, and Allan Loughead became its West Coast distributor. But he continued to dream of airplanes.

Allan would meet from time to time with Northrop to share thoughts on a possible future project, a cabin monoplane with an enclosed cockpit and a cantilevered wing mounted atop a monocoque fuselage. In 1926, the two visionaries managed to secure $25,000 in backing for their project and set up shop in Hollywood. Because the principal backer wanted a clear association with Malcolm's respected brake company, the designers named the firm the Lockheed Aircraft Company.

The Lockheed prototype was completed the following summer. Northrop named it the Vega, after one of the sky's brightest stars. From its first flight on July 4, the new plane was a huge success. In 1928, the third

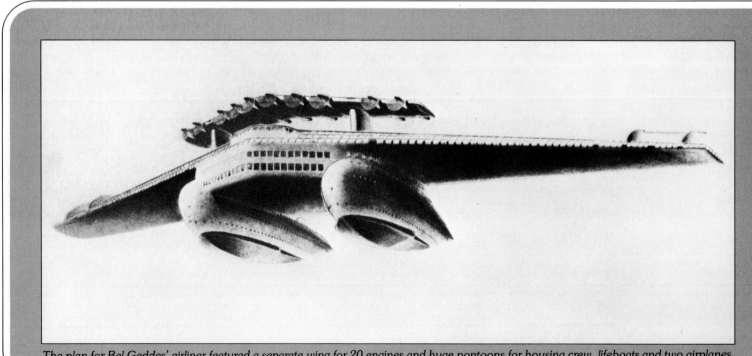

The plan for Bel Geddes' airliner featured a separate wing for 20 engines and huge pontoons for housing crew, lifeboats and two airplanes.

Vega built took Australian explorer George Hubert Wilkins from Alaska to Norway, the first trans-Arctic flight, and then on the first flight over Antarctica. Wiley Post set two round-the-world speed records in his Vega, the *Winnie Mae,* in 1931 and 1933, and Amelia Earhart became the first woman to fly solo across the Atlantic and nonstop across the United States in her Vega in 1932.

By that time, the Vega had realized its high-speed potential. The 450-horsepower Pratt & Whitney Wasp C, first available in 1929, and such modifications as a NACA engine cowling and streamlined wheel pants for the landing gear enabled it to cruise at 160 miles per hour. Thus equipped, the plane consistently defeated specialized racing aircraft in cross-country competition. The press called the new airplane the "plywood bullet" and gave currency to the slogan, "It takes a Lockheed to beat a Lockheed."

The first Vega had scarcely flown when Jack Northrop began changing the design's wing position to create two noticeably different aircraft. The first was the Air Express, an accommodation to the preferences of veteran airmail pilots for open cockpits positioned well back of the wing. Shifting the cockpit from the front of the Vega's cabin to an opening near the tail was simple enough, but the Vega's high wing would then have limited the pilot's forward visibility. So the wing was raised on short struts to create a parasol monoplane that provided a good view to the front. Detaching the wing from the fuselage also exposed a few more feet of wing surface, giving the Air Express extra lift and thus a greater payload than the Vega.

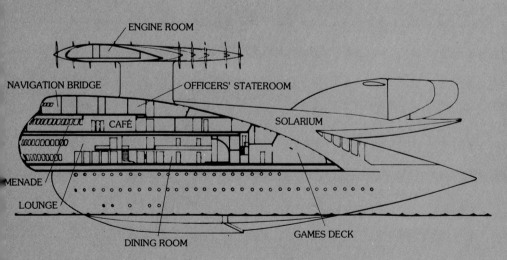

The great craft was to have nine decks, four of which are shown here in cross section. Planned luxury features included a dance floor, a gymnasium, a 200-seat dining room and an enclosed promenade deck.

An impossible dream of fabulous luxury

Industrial designer Norman Bel Geddes loved challenges; the tougher they were, the more they appealed to him. In 1929 he exhorted his staff to find a way of getting "a thousand luxury lovers from New York to Paris fast." The result—on paper—was a 700-ton airliner with a 577-foot wingspan, a crew of 155 and accommodations for 451 passengers.

Bel Geddes believed his 90-mile-an-hour behemoth could compete with the ocean liners of the day since it could make three Atlantic crossings a week to their one. But the plane's nine-million-dollar price tag discouraged investors, and it died on the drawing board.

The second distinct aircraft to evolve from the Vega was the Sirius. Built to the specifications of Charles Lindbergh, who wanted a plane for himself and his wife, Anne, the Sirius had tandem, open cockpits. At Anne Lindbergh's request, the plane was fitted with sliding canopies to cover the drafty cockpits. But more significant than the cockpit arrangement was the position of the wing. In his initial design work on the plane, Northrop chose not to raise the wing for visibility but to lower it, attaching it to the bottom of the fuselage. When completed in 1929, the Sirius became the first American, commercial low-wing monoplane. By that time, however, Northrop had left Lockheed to start his own firm. There he would turn out a series of all-metal low-wing monoplanes that, to no one's surprise, resembled his last design for Lockheed.

The loss of Northrop was a serious blow but not a devastating one to the young company. Under his successors, first Gerard Vultee and later Richard van Hake, Lockheed completed work on the Sirius and developed the Orion, the fourth major aircraft to use the basic Vega airframe.

The Orion restored the pilot to the enclosed, forward position he occupied in the Vega and featured a Vega-type six-seat passenger cabin behind him. The low wing of the Sirius was retained in the Orion because it offered a convenient space into which the landing gear could be retracted. The Orion was the first commercial aircraft to provide retractable gear as standard equipment. That single feature added 30 miles per hour to its top speed, which at 225 miles per hour was by far the fastest of any airliner and significantly better than most contemporary single-seat fighter planes. The superiority of the Orion and its distinguished predecessors was widely recognized, but by the time the new plane went into production, Lockheed Aircraft was on the verge of bankruptcy, a victim of the Depression.

The decline had begun in 1929 when Allan Lockheed and his backers were bought out by a large holding and manufacturing company called Detroit Aircraft Corporation. At the time, Detroit Aircraft nurtured ambitions of becoming the General Motors of the air. But after the stock market crash, when many of its other ventures began to fail, the firm started to siphon profits from the Lockheed division to support the rest of the company. Eventually the whole corporation collapsed in a welter of bankruptcy suits, and the Lockheed division went into re-

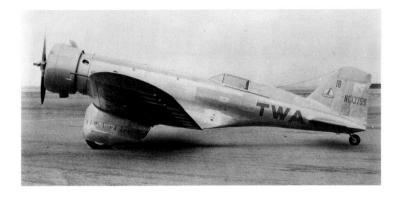

In the early 1930s, the monoplane became the dominant trend in aircraft design. The Northrop Alpha (far left) revived all-metal wing construction, while the Lockheed Orion (left) was the first commercial transport with retractable landing gear. The Northrop Gamma (above) was used by Trans World Airlines for high-altitude research, and the Boeing 247 (right) became the first modern twin-engined airliner.

ceivership. In July of 1932, Lockheed's assets were purchased for a mere $40,000 by an investment banker from San Francisco.

The banker, Robert Gross, headed a consortium of aviation enthusiasts who wanted to build a new generation of airliners under the Lockheed name. Yet they were not sure what form their new planes should take, until Boeing Aircraft of Seattle introduced its revolutionary Model 247 airliner in February of 1933. Like Lockheed's Orion, the Model 247 was a low-wing monoplane with a monocoque fuselage, cantilevered wings and retractable landing gear. But it was made almost entirely of metal rather than wood, and it had the added margin of power and safety provided by two engines. It carried 10 passengers—four more than the Orion—plus a pilot, copilot and stewardess, and it provided a galley, a lavatory and space for baggage and mail. The Model 247 was the first modern airliner, and as soon as Robert Gross saw one, he knew the direction in which he wanted Lockheed to move.

He ordered work stopped on a single-engined transport that was in an advanced stage of development and had the engineering staff concentrate its efforts on enlarging a twin-engined craft then taking shape on the drawing board. Under the guidance of Hall Hibbard, a graduate of M.I.T. and head of engineering, a scale model of the new plane was completed in just eight months and shipped from the Lockheed plant at Burbank to the University of Michigan for wind-tunnel tests.

A short time later, a young aeronautical engineer named Clarence L. "Kelly" Johnson, who worked at the tunnel, reported by telephone to Lockheed. The tests revealed a serious problem: The model's rudder would not provide sufficient control if the plane had to be flown with one engine. Johnson thought he could fix the tail. Hibbard listened to his proposal, and Johnson was soon hard at work in Burbank; it was the beginning of a long and distinguished career at Lockheed. In a few weeks, Johnson had replaced the single vertical fin and rudder of the original model with twin vertical fins attached to the tips of the horizontal stabilizer. Johnson loaded the redesigned model in his car and drove back to Ann Arbor for more tests. The new tail worked. Construction began almost immediately, and the first 10-passenger Lockheed Electra was ready to fly early in 1934.

Veteran Lockheed test pilot Marshall Headle took the Electra up for

A wellspring of advances in flight

In July 1917, three months after the United States entered World War I, construction of a laboratory building began on a tract of farmland near Hampton, Virginia. The site was called Langley Field, and the building was the first of a sprawling complex of laboratories, wind tunnels and offices *(right)* that would house the most important flight research center in the world, the National Advisory Committee for Aeronautics (NACA).

NACA had been legislated by Congress in 1915 to "direct the scientific study of the problems of flight, with a view to their practical solution." It was a belated response to the aviation advances made by government-funded research centers in Europe. But NACA quickly made up for lost time. In the 1920s and '30s, Langley scientists developed a series of innovative wind tunnels that permitted measurements of unprecedented accuracy with both small models and full-scale aircraft.

The work at Langley made NACA world-famous. An engine cowling developed there dramatically reduced drag and improved cooling on radial engines. Langley-designed airfoils increased the lift of wings and the thrust of propellers on scores of designs. And NACA research proved conclusively that the reduced drag of a retractable landing gear more than compensated for the weight of the mechanisms needed to operate it.

NACA's studies extended beyond basic aerodynamics to such details as wing deicing, the spacing of cooling fins on engine cylinders and shaving off the heads of rivets to improve streamlining. So far-reaching were the achievements of scientists at Langley that one British expert complained in 1935 that "our most capable design staffs base their technical work upon the results of the American NACA."

An engine cowling undergoes a wind-tunnel test in 1929. A cowling alone could boost a plane's speed by as much as 20 mph.

An auxiliary airfoil, being tested as an antistall device, projects from the parasol wing of a 1932 Fairchild 22.

A 1934 experimental plane is equipped with NACA's steerable tricycle landing gear to improve control while taxiing.

its first tests on February 23 and found that the new plane would cruise at 190 miles per hour and had a top speed of better than 200. A few days later, Headle ran the Electra through tests required for certification by the Civil Aeronautics Authority and was about to land when he noticed that the left wheel would not come down. Employees who had gathered on the Lockheed airfield to welcome the triumphant prototype now watched anxiously as the crippled craft, on which all their futures depended, prepared for a crash landing.

Headle knew that serious damage to the prototype would at the very least delay production. Moreover, a landing mishap might lead potential customers to see the plane as unreliable. Headle tried everything he could think of to get the left gear down, diving the plane repeatedly and pulling up sharply in hopes that inertia would pop the wheel free. But it remained stubbornly tucked up in the wing. A mechanic on board for the certification tests chiseled a hole in the fuselage wall just behind the main wing spar and crawled into the cramped space inside the wing to try pushing the wheel down, but he could not reach it.

Headle dropped a note to the waiting crowd: What should he do now? His answer was a message chalked on the body of an Orion that flew up to meet him: "Try landing at Union—Good luck." Union Air Terminal, a mile away, had a longer runway than the Lockheed field and better fire-fighting equipment. Approaching the Union runway,

Designed for fast, economical operation, the twin-engined, twin-tailed Lockheed Electra could carry 10 passengers and a crew of two. With a price tag of only $35,000, it was the least expensive airliner of its day; a total of 148 were built between 1934 and 1941.

Headle drained the remaining fuel from his tanks and eased the Electra down to a gentle one-wheel landing. As the plane slowed, its left wing tip fell to the runway. The craft pivoted around the wing tip in a ground loop and came to a stop. Headle's skill had restricted damage to the wing tip, which was quickly repaired; the defect in the landing gear was corrected, and orders poured in. The new Lockheed was more than a match for the Boeing 247, and while it carried four fewer passengers than the Douglas DC-2, which was introduced a few months later, it cost less than half as much. And in the best Lockheed tradition, it was faster.

Fast as the Electra was, it had been designed, like all airliners, with reliability and load-carrying efficiency as primary considerations. But in another, more specialized breed of aircraft—racing planes—speed was the overriding consideration. Range, reliability, maneuverability—all were sacrificed to velocity. Even so, some of the innovations that made these planes fast were later applied to conventional aircraft.

Of all the competition planes of the 1930s, the one that best exhibited the practical potential of high-speed design features was the custom-built racing machine of a young Texas-born millionaire named Howard Robard Hughes. The Hughes Racer never flew as fast in a straight sprint as two great floatplane racers, the British Supermarine S.6B and the Italian Macchi-Castoldi M.C.72, both of which topped 400 miles per hour in the early 1930s. But with less than a third of the floatplanes' power, the Hughes Racer set a transcontinental speed record that the two faster planes could not have attempted to match. They were powered by racing engines tuned to run for just minutes between overhauls; Hughes's plane was equipped with a standard production power plant and got its speed from simple aerodynamic refinements that were applicable to everyday aircraft.

Howard Hughes had inherited his fortune from his father, Howard Sr., who died in 1924 when his son was 18. The elder Hughes had invented a uniquely effective bit for drilling oil wells and founded the Hughes Tool Company in Houston to manufacture it. Soon after young Howard took over the firm, he turned day-to-day operations over to a group of managers and left for Hollywood to make movies. Over the next two years he bankrolled one flop and three hits. Then, after Lindbergh's momentous flight in 1927, Hughes, like many others in Hollywood, decided to make an aviation picture. He called it *Hell's Angels.*

Hughes had taken his first ride in an airplane at the age of 13 and had been enthralled with flying ever since. He had taken flying lessons on several occasions, and by the time shooting began on his World War I aviation epic he was an accomplished pilot. His intense interest in the subject of his new movie prompted him to take an unusually active role in the production, and his interference drove two directors to quit the project in quick succession. The second, as he walked out, remarked to Hughes, "If you know so much, why don't you direct it yourself?"

Hughes did, lavishing special care on the film's now-celebrated aerial combat sequences. By the time *Hell's Angels* was finished in 1930, it had cost Hughes almost four million dollars, far more than had ever been spent on a movie before, and reportedly more than it earned at the box office despite long runs and packed houses.

Having had enough of film making for a while, Hughes began to focus his attention on high-speed aircraft. A year earlier he had bought a Boeing F4B-1, the Navy's new biplane fighter. The stubby plane satisfied him in every regard but one: Its 185-mile-per-hour top speed was not fast enough. He took the plane to Douglas and later to Lockheed for modifications to the airframe and engine that would reduce drag and increase speed. At Lockheed, Hughes met Richard Palmer, who had designed the Orion's retractable landing gear. The two became friends and spent many hours in Lockheed's hangars talking airplanes.

In January 1934, Hughes entered the souped-up fighter in the All American Air Meet, flying it in the Sportsman-Pilot's Free-For-All. Over the 20-mile, four-lap race with tight turns around pylons, the Boeing's average speed matched its former top speed of 185 miles per hour, and Hughes won so easily he almost lapped his nearest competitor.

But even after his triumph, Hughes continued to suggest more and more modifications for the Boeing. Finally his exasperated mechanic, Glenn Odekirk, exclaimed, "Howard, why don't you build your own plane from scratch? That's the only way you'll ever be satisfied." And once again Hughes took to heart a comment intended as sarcasm.

Hughes kept up with the latest developments in aviation and had an intuitive grasp of what would work on an aircraft, but he was no designer. For that job, he hired Dick Palmer, inviting him by telegram to design "the fastest plane in the world." Palmer accepted and began work in Los Angeles on what came to be called the Hughes Racer.

Hughes did not hesitate to offer his own suggestions—or to reject those of his designer. Palmer, for his part, developed an admiration for Hughes's methods of operation. "Howard was the greatest brain picker I ever saw," he later recalled. "He'd disappear for a few days and go to NACA. There, he'd drink coffee with the government's top engineers and flight designers. He'd find out what he wanted to know then fly home, tell us, and our problem would be solved."

Gradually the Racer took shape. Like most new aircraft of 1934, it would be a low-wing cantilevered monoplane with an aluminum-alloy monocoque fuselage. For a power plant, Palmer chose a reliable, air-cooled radial, the Pratt & Whitney Twin Wasp. It produced 700 horsepower from 14 cylinders, which were arranged in two banks, one behind the other, minimizing wind resistance. As on all racers, the wings would be short to cut down on drag, but they would have to be carefully shaped to provide enough lift to get the plane off the ground with a takeoff run of manageable length. The Racer was to be a land plane and would not have a floatplane's luxury of a limitless runway.

Palmer refined the plane's basic configuration by testing models with various wing and fuselage shapes in the wind tunnel at the California

Suiting up for the stratosphere

For decades after the Wright brothers' first flight, most flying was confined to the atmosphere a few thousand feet above the ground. For those who dared go higher, there were dangers. In 1934, Italy's Renato Donati reached a record altitude of 47,352 feet but afterward was carried from his plane in shock. The atmospheric pressure at such heights was simply too low for the body to tolerate.

Then, that same year, test pilot Wiley Post found a solution. He commissioned the B. F. Goodrich Company to create the first practical pressurized flying suit *(below)*. Wearing it, he soared to almost 50,000 feet with no ill effects in tests that foreshadowed the day when flights into the stratosphere would be routine.

Seated beside his Lockheed Vega, Wiley Post wears the rubber-and-cloth flight suit he used for high-altitude tests in 1934. Pressure was monitored by the gauge he holds in his right hand.

Institute of Technology. The tests led to the design of a remarkably short, 25-foot wing with a sophisticated airfoil developed at NACA, a rounded tip and a pronounced taper. The fuselage was to be unusually slim for its length, with its largest diameter at the engine.

Next, Palmer turned to the finer details of the design. It was there that Hughes's limitless funds and obsessive attention to minutiae, together with Palmer's genius, produced truly innovative refinements. The landing gear, Palmer's specialty at Lockheed, retracted completely into wheel wells in the bottom of the wing and was sealed with landing-gear doors that fitted flush with the wing's under surface. On most planes, retracted wheels remained partly exposed, causing drag that Palmer's design eliminated. Even the tail skid pulled up neatly into the fuselage.

The radial engine was tightly sheathed in a new drag-reducing bell-shaped cowling. The propeller incorporated a hydraulic mechanism, newly perfected by the Hamilton-Standard Company, that altered the pitch of the blades in flight to make maximum use of engine power at different air speeds. The engine itself featured another novelty—a nozzle-like exhaust aimed toward the rear to contribute extra thrust—and its oil was cooled by air funneled through small, efficient ducts on the leading edges of the wings, yet another first.

The aluminum-alloy skin of the fuselage was riveted to the frame as usual, but instead of overlapping adjoining sheets of aluminum, workmen butted them end to end for the smoothest surface possible, then they carefully shaved down the head of each rivet so that not the slightest bump remained to disturb the flow of air. Even flat screwheads were set so that their slots aligned with the airflow.

Palmer wanted the wings even smoother than the fuselage, so he had their framework covered with oversized sheets of plywood that were then trimmed, shaved and sanded to a perfect contour. Finely woven fabric, stretched over the plywood, then sealed, doped, painted and waxed, gave the wing a glass-smooth surface. Elegantly curved fillets joined wing and fuselage to prevent the formation of turbulence that could buffet the tail.

By the time the Racer was completed in August 1935, Hughes had spent more than $100,000 on it. What he got for his money—and effort—was by general acknowledgment the world's most aerodynamically refined and meticulously crafted airplane.

Over the objections of fearful Hughes Tool executives, Hughes took the Racer up on its first flight at Mines Field in Los Angeles on August 18, 1935. The gleaming plane lifted nimbly off the runway in spite of its short wings, and Hughes eased it through a quick test, holding the speed down to 250 miles per hour. He noted that the variable-pitch propeller was not working properly and made a smooth landing after 15 minutes, taxiing up to the waiting Hughes team, who burst into spontaneous applause. "She flies fine," he said as he climbed out of the cockpit. He instructed mechanics to check the propeller, then turned to Palmer and said, "I think we can do it. Let's try."

"It" was the world's speed record for land planes. The rules for such an attempt, established by the Fédération Aéronautique Internationale (F.A.I.), the official keeper of world air records, were demanding ones. Under the watchful eye of America's National Aeronautical Association, Hughes would have to make two upwind and two downwind passes over a three-kilometer course at no more than 60 meters (less than 200 feet) above ground. Photoelectric timers would measure his speed. The existing record was 314.319 miles per hour, set the previous December by the French pilot Raymonde Delmotte in a Caudron C-460. Reportedly, the French government had provided a million-dollar subsidy for the plane's construction. To establish a new record, Hughes would have to beat Delmotte's mark on each of four passes. His average for the four passes would become the new speed record.

In early September, after two more shakedown flights, Hughes was ready for the record attempt. On the afternoon of the 12th he flew the Racer from its hangar in Burbank to a measured course officials had set up at the Santa Ana Airport in Orange County.

The next morning, Amelia Earhart and fellow pilot Paul Mantz, a stunt-flying veteran of *Hell's Angels,* took off in Earhart's Lockheed Vega, climbed to 1,000 feet and circled there. They were to act as altitude judges; under F.A.I. rules, Hughes could climb no higher than 1,000 feet before beginning his dive toward the course, which had to be traversed in level flight. Hughes took off, climbed to the allowable altitude and quickly made the regulation four passes over the course. He then made two more to be sure he had four that clearly eclipsed the old mark. He was about to climb and turn for a seventh when the Racer's engine abruptly quit. The main fuel supply was exhausted. When Hughes tried to switch to the reserve tank, nothing happened, so he let the speeding, powerless plane climb until it was on the verge of a stall. Then he turned skillfully into the wind to set up a dead-stick landing.

It was soon clear that the Racer did not have sufficient altitude to glide to the airfield, so Hughes prepared to put down in a plowed beet field nearby. He left the landing gear up lest the lowered wheels dig into the soft earth at touchdown and flip the plane. Observers on the course saw the plane descend rapidly with its wheels up and then disappear in a cloud of dust. Fearing the worst, they jumped into their cars and raced to the site. There they found the Racer on its belly in the middle of the beet field. Its propeller was bent and its fuselage scratched, but it was otherwise undamaged. Hughes sat on the fuselage scribbling in a notebook. He looked at his rescuers with a grin and asked, "Did I make it?"

He had indeed. His average speed of 352.388 miles per hour obliterated the old record. Almost immediately Hughes's team began to repair the Racer and give it a new, longer wing so that the plane could lift a greater fuel load for an attempt at another record—the fastest flight from coast to coast. The Racer was ready to go again late in 1936, and the following January Hughes flew it from Burbank to Newark in 7 hours 28 minutes and 25 seconds for an average speed of 327.1 miles per hour. Hughes's record, which shattered the previous one by nearly two hours, would stand for seven years.

For his next record attempt, a try at the fastest round-the-world flight, Hughes turned to Lockheed's successor to the Electra, the Model 14 airliner. The plane incorporated a few advances that Hughes had pioneered on the Racer, such as bell-shaped engine cowlings and some flush riveting in critical areas. After weeks of preparation, Hughes, copilot Harry Connor and a crew of three took off from New York's Floyd Bennett Field at 7:20 p.m. on July 10, 1938. They headed east, stopping first in Paris, then crossing Europe and the Soviet Union. Flying over the Bering Strait to Alaska, they arrived back at Floyd Bennett Field at 2:37 p.m. on July 14. Elapsed time: 3 days 19 hours and 17 minutes, half the previous record. It would be nine years before anyone took less time to circle the globe.

But more important than the record was the precision with which the flight had been executed. A production aircraft had flown around the world almost exactly as planned. Hughes had made no unscheduled stops and had scarcely deviated from his plotted course. The flight was a spectacular demonstration, not so much of the speed of the modern airplane but of its reliability as a means of long-distance transportation. It dramatized the great advances made in airliner performance in the decade following the introduction of the Lockheed Vega—advances not lost on the public: Passenger traffic on U.S. airlines doubled in the closing years of the decade. But by then, the designers and test pilots who had wrought the transformation in civilian aviation were already focusing their attention on a new generation of warplanes. ᐧᐧ

By far the most advanced design of the mid-1930s, Howard Hughes's Racer displays the sleek lines that helped make it the fastest landplane of its day at 352 mph. Its basic configuration was later adopted by World War II fighters such as the Mitsubishi Type 0 (Zero), the Focke-Wulf Fw 190 and the Republic P-47 Thunderbolt.

The woman who flew for the Reich

Among the brave and brilliant test pilots of World War II, Germany's Hanna Reitsch was a sterling example—an aviator distinguished by her profound love of flight, coupled with iron self-discipline and consummate skill.

Reitsch started her flying career in gliders in the province of Silesia in 1931. Almost from her first flight, it was evident that the diminutive teenager—who weighed less than 90 pounds and stood a half inch over five feet—was a gifted natural pilot. Three years later she gained admission to the previously all-male Civil Airways Training School, where she learned to fly a variety of powered aircraft. To gain a thorough understanding of mechanics, she even dismantled the engine of her first plane and reassembled it.

In 1937, the 25-year-old Reitsch became a test pilot for the Luftwaffe. She flew virtually every new craft that the fertile German aviation industry developed—seaplane gliders, bombers, fighters and helicopters. Reitsch demonstrated such skill that in late 1942 she was chosen to fly the skittery Me 163B rocket plane. On one flight, she was forced into a crash landing that left her with multiple skull fractures. As rescue workers struggled to pry her from the plane's wreckage, she fought to remain conscious until she had written down her observations "so the flight might not have been in vain."

After several months of painful convalescence, Reitsch took to the air once more. And in February 1944, she proposed Operation *Suicide,* a program in which pilots were to steer V-1 flying bombs—launched from bombers and equipped with cockpits—directly at enemy cities and factories. Reitsch herself made 10 test flights in the V-1 without accident—and was the only one of seven pilots not killed or seriously injured in the jet-powered craft. In June 1944, the Allied invasion of Europe ended Operation *Suicide* and Reitsch resumed testing conventional aircraft.

When the War ended, Reitsch was stripped of her pilot's licenses. She later regained her sports pilot's license and became an instructor, but she could never find another job as a test pilot. She died at the age of 67 in 1979 without again doing the work she loved best—"introducing the plane for the first time into its element."

As a beaming Adolf Hitler looks on, Hanna Reitsch examines a certificate marking his 1942 award to her of the Iron Cross First Class. The only woman to receive the medal, Reitsch was honored for her test flights in the dangerously unstable Me 163B rocket plane.

A 21-year-old Hanna Reitsch proudly displays her Grunau-Baby training glider before the famed Rhön Soaring Contests in Germany in 1933. Reitsch did not win any event, but her overall performance earned her a spot on a tour of South America by Germany's best glider pilots.

Her glider towed by a winch-driven line, Reitsch takes off from a field in Finland in 1934. The Finnish government had invited Reitsch and other German pilots to teach gliding, which the Finns took to "with eager enthusiasm," she reported.

At the 1937 Rhön Soaring Contests, Reitsch — soon to be a Luftwaffe test pilot — enthusiastically explains gliding techniques to British pilot Joan Pric

Steadied from below, Reitsch settles designer Heinrich Focke's Fa-61 helicopter gently to the ground after a 1937 test flight.

Gliding onto a frame of braking cables, Reitsch completes a 1940 dry run of a system for landing aircraft on ships' decks.

Reitsch waves from the cockpit of an He 111 bomber—one of many planes she tested at Rechlin, a base in northern Germany.

During 1942, Reitsch test-flew the Me 163B rocket plane, an aircraft in which she suffered a near-fatal crash.

Fitted with wooden wings, a V-1 of the type Reitsch flew in 1944 maintains level flight after release from a bomber.

Reitsch banks a Fieseler S___h, a plane she later flew under fire into Berlin during the ___ itch defense of the city in 1945.

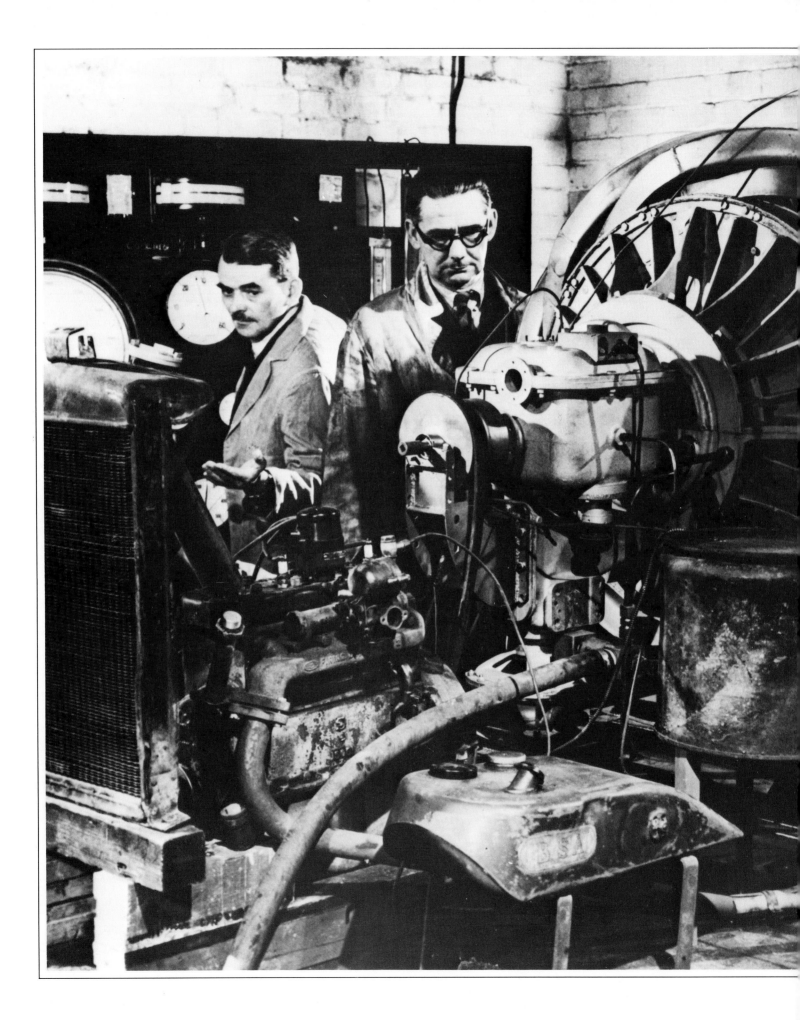

3
Forging weapons of aerial warfare

In the 1930s, as the airplane developed into a practical means of civilian transportation, the precarious political order established after World War I began to teeter. Germany and Japan took belligerent stances, and nations around the world looked to their defenses. New military planes of every description took shape on the drawing boards of aircraft designers.

The most spectacular of these warbirds were the fighters. A fighter had to be maneuverable and it had to be able to climb quickly, but it also had to possess superior speed. In an air battle the faster fighter could dictate the terms of combat—and escape if the situation got out of hand. Yet to combine these attributes in a single aircraft was a daunting task for even the most accomplished designers.

In the scramble for speed, the men who made the engines became behind-the-scenes heroes. Through simple determination and inspired resourcefulness, they squeezed undreamed-of horsepower from their assemblages of churning pistons and clattering valves. However, there were limits to what the piston engine could achieve. When its potential had been exhausted, designers were to turn to a radically different kind of power plant—the turbojet.

Military aviation in Germany had been severely restricted by the Treaty of Versailles. An Air Ministry and the building of cargo and passenger planes were permitted, but a German air force had been outlawed. Yet even before Hitler came to power, Germany had begun to rebuild its air arm by training pilots in glider clubs and in secret classes at commercial flying schools, and by illegally establishing a closet air staff. In 1934, the secrecy shrouding the Luftwaffe dissipated when the Air Ministry invited Germany's best aircraft manufacturers—Ernst Heinkel A.G., Bayerische Flugzeugwerke (BFW) and Focke-Wulf among them—to enter a competition to design a new fighter. In March 1934, Willy Messerschmitt, then working at BFW, began drafting the angular outline of his Bf 109. It would be widely known as the Me, or Messerschmitt, 109.

Messerschmitt had first made a name for himself in 1924 as a young designer with big ideas and a tiny company in Bamberg. His M.17 was a

Frank Whittle (far left), who pioneered the development of the turbojet in Great Britain during the 1930s, works with an assistant on the first of his engines, the so-called Whittle Unit, or WU.

A Messerschmitt 109 fighter lands after a mission in 1943. Between 1935 and 1945, Messerschmitt produced more than 33,000 of the single-seat aircraft, making the Me 109 one of the most widely manufactured combat planes of World War II.

high-wing monoplane that resembled a two-seat glider with an engine attached; the little sport plane weighed only 200 pounds, but with its 25-horsepower engine and 52-foot wingspan, it could lift twice its own weight. Only two were built, but knowledgeable aviation men in Germany were impressed. Three years later, Messerschmitt's M.19, a low-wing single seater, won him a cash prize of 60,000 reichsmarks, which Messerschmitt used to purchase part ownership in BFW.

Messerschmitt's first major project at BFW was the Me 109. In May 1935, just 15 months after he set pencil to paper, a prototype of the world's most advanced fighter to date stood on the tarmac, ready for flight. It was only 28 feet long and had a wingspan of barely 32½ feet—just big enough to carry aloft a pilot and a battery of machine guns.

Except for the ailerons, elevators and rudder, which were covered with fabric, the Me 109 was constructed entirely of metal. The aluminum skin was flush-riveted to the fuselage and wings to reduce drag. Handley Page slats *(page 42)* were attached to the leading edge of the wing; at low speeds they opened automatically to lower the plane's stalling speed and to give the pilot better control. The plane was supported on a retractable landing gear that was operated by hand crank. An enclosed cockpit, a novelty for fighters of the day, protected the pilot from the elements. Individually, these features were of little note; all had been used before on other airplanes. But Willy Messerschmitt was the first designer to combine them in a fighter.

The responsibility for trying out the new plane rested with 27-year-old Hans Knötsch, BFW's chief pilot. Pulling on the white leather gloves that were his trademark, Knötsch squeezed into the narrow cockpit and warmed up the engine. Ironically, the engine was of British manufacture, a 695-horsepower Kestrel built by Rolls-Royce; German engines of comparable power would not be ready for months. After several taxiing runs to get the feel of the plane, Knötsch took off, furiously cranking with one hand to retract the undercarriage.

Twenty minutes later, Knötsch landed, taxied to a halt and emerged from the cockpit wearing a grin that broadcast his satisfaction with the plane. He had reservations about the landing gear; the wheels were so close together that the aircraft could tip onto a wing when rolling across a rough sod fighter strip. But in the air, the Me 109 had handled superbly. Still, it was not enough for Knötsch to be enthusiastic; he was, after all, BFW's pilot. The Air Ministry had to be convinced of the plane's superiority in a fly-off against the aircraft of the other manufacturers that had been invited to enter the fighter competition. Air Ministry officials would see for themselves which aircraft had superior speed, rate of climb and maneuverability. The event was scheduled for October 1935.

Perhaps the best known of the competing firms was Heinkel. The company entered its He 112, an open-cockpit monoplane slightly larger and heavier than the Me 109. Focke-Wulf entered the Fw 159, a parasol fighter. Arado, the fourth builder, came to the contest with the Ar 80, a low-wing monoplane and the only entry with a fixed undercarriage.

The fly-off got under way, and the Arado was soon eliminated as a contender; the wheels, extending into the slip stream, caused too much drag for it to fly as fast as the other planes. Next to drop out was the Fw 159. The system for retracting its landing gear, complex and prone to failure, malfunctioned, and the plane's speed proved disappointing.

That left only the He 112 and the Me 109. They were so similar in performance that the contest ended in a draw, with the Air Ministry ordering 10 prototypes of each for further testing. By late 1936, however, the issue had been decided in favor of the Me 109, not because it could fly faster, turn sharper or climb higher, but because it would be simpler to mass-produce; the angular lines of the Me 109 were easier to fabricate than the curves of Heinkel's design. The Luftwaffe took delivery of the first squadrons of the fighter in the spring of 1937.

One of the few foreign pilots to try out the new plane—and the first American to do so—was Al Williams, onetime holder of the world's speed record. Flying through Europe on a promotional tour for Gulf Oil, Williams struck a deal with General Ernst Udet, a friend of his who had been an ace in World War I and who now directed the Luftwaffe's Technical Office. Williams would let Udet fly his bright orange Grumman biplane if he could fly Udet's Messerschmitt.

Williams was favorably impressed from the moment the engine coughed to life. By this time a Daimler-Benz of 910 horsepower had replaced the British Kestrel. Williams took off and, after getting the feel of the controls, began to put the Me 109 through a punishing sequence of aerobatics. The plane not only performed the maneuvers flawlessly but proved to be a remarkably stable gun platform. The trigger was on

Designer Willy Messerschmitt congratulates Fritz Wendel after the test pilot set a world speed record of 469.2 mph in April 1939. To bolster the image of the Luftwaffe, propagandists announced that Wendel had set the record in the Me 109, by then Germany's standard fighter. In fact, he had flown the Me 209, a speedy experimental plane that was never manufactured.

the control stick, and a slight pressure set the fighter's three machine guns to chattering. "It was the final little detail," said Williams, "that brought me the impression that instead of flying an airplane upon which guns were mounted, I was actually aiming a delicately balanced rifle."

The Luftwaffe was justifiably proud of its new Messerschmitt, but far from smug about it. The undercarriage was fragile. Moreover, the torque from the engine made the plane veer alarmingly to port on takeoff. With practice, a pilot could use the rudder to straighten the plane, but the characteristic would never be completely remedied.

More worrisome was the Messerschmitt's meager armament. The Luftwaffe had no one to blame but itself for this; in its original specifications it had called for only two 7.92-millimeter machine guns. Messerschmitt had managed to squeeze a third into early production models. But German spies were now reporting that the British were developing fighters that carried four machine guns. Their information was incorrect; Britain's new planes, in fact, possessed eight .303-caliber guns.

The Royal Air Force had demanded this massive arsenal for the soundest of reasons: As fighters flew faster and faster, more and more firepower would be necessary to compensate for the shorter time a pilot would have in which to shoot. Yet ironically, the RAF for years had lagged behind the Luftwaffe in acquiring the very fighters that would make eight guns indispensable. In 1931, the British Air Staff had asked the nation's aircraft industry to come up with designs that would have exceptional speed, both in climbing to combat altitude and in flying straight and level. At that time the standard engines could produce about 650 horsepower; thus the top speed of even the most streamlined aircraft was limited to 250 miles per hour or so. A monoplane so powered would face stiff competition from a well-designed biplane. The biplane might be slightly slower, but with two wings rather than one, it would be able to climb faster and maneuver with greater agility.

Of the eight designs submitted to the Air Staff, five were biplanes. One of these, the Gloster Gladiator, won government approval, and hundreds were ordered by the RAF. Among the three monoplanes entered was the Supermarine Type 224, of which much was expected, if for no other reason than that it was created by Reginald Mitchell, the speed king of designers.

Mitchell had joined the Supermarine Aviation works in Southampton in 1916, after apprenticing as an engineer in a locomotive factory. He advanced rapidly to chief designer of the company and by the late 1920s his success with his Schneider Cup racers—seaplanes whose sole purpose was speed—had made him the envy of the aviation world.

Yet his Type 224 was a flop; the Gloster Gladiator could not only outclimb and outturn it, but even outspeed it by four miles per hour. Beverly Shenstone, a young aeronautical engineer who came to work for Mitchell at about this time, commented on the debacle: "The design team had done so well with racing float planes that they thought it would

A de Havilland Mosquito light bomber cruises above the clouds in 1942, shortly after the plane went into service with the RAF. Built of wood as an economy measure, the Mosquito, with a top speed of more than 400 mph, was as fast as the speediest all-metal fighters of the day, yet simpler to build and faster to repair.

be child's play to design a fighter intended to fly at little over half that speed. They never made that mistake again.''

Mitchell set about at once redesigning the 224. He shortened the wings and fuselage to trim the plane by 250 pounds, but it was still two feet longer and had a wingspan four feet wider than the Me 109. Mitchell also gave his plane a retractable landing gear to reduce drag. Though the aircraft, which Supermarine now called the Type 300, would thus gain 30 miles per hour in speed, it would climb more slowly than the Type 224 because the wings were smaller. The Air Staff remained unimpressed. But in the autumn of 1934, Supermarine concluded an agreement with Rolls-Royce for a brand-new engine. It was the Merlin, named for a small but fierce European falcon, and it could turn the Type 300 into a full-fledged bird of prey.

At about the same time, Sidney Camm, Hawker Aircraft's premier designer, settled on the Merlin for his own monoplane fighter, the Hurricane. While the Type 300 was to be built using the latest monocoque construction techniques, Camm designed the Hurricane with a metal-and-wooden structure covered mostly in fabric. Although his plane

Workers fit a wooden propeller to an early Spitfire. Later, variable-pitch metal props improved the plane's speed, acceleration and rate of climb.

would not match the 300's performance, it could be ready sooner, a factor that persuaded the RAF to order 600 Hurricanes in June 1936.

On the test stand the Merlin had shown that it was capable of producing nearly 800 horsepower, 140 more than the Rolls-Royce Goshawk in the Type 224. Rolls-Royce saw few obstacles to increasing the Merlin's output by 25 per cent. With power of this magnitude at his disposal, Mitchell calculated that his fighter could fly faster than 300 miles per hour and that its rate of climb would exceed the Gladiator's. The Air Ministry took notice and in April 1935 signed a contract with Supermarine for an experimental fighter armed with six or eight machine guns. The result was one of the most famous of all planes, the Spitfire.

When completed the following summer, the Spitfire exhibited an elegance of line that still appeals to connoisseurs of fine aircraft. It was less angular than the Me 109 and flew on graceful, elliptical wings. The elliptical wing, because it did not begin to taper until near the tip, had space to fit four guns in each wing. Moreover, for its length the elliptical shape had a greater area than a conventional wing; it could be thinner to reduce drag without sacrificing lift.

In addition, the Spitfire incorporated an entirely new radiator, invented by F. W. Meredith at the Royal Aircraft Establishment (formerly the Royal Aircraft Factory). Aircraft radiators perforce extended below the fuselage into the slip stream, increasing drag considerably. But Meredith designed a duct for his radiator that accelerated the air passing through it. The result was enough thrust to overcome the radiator's drag.

The Spitfire performed so well during its first flight, on March 5, 1936, that Supermarine test pilot Joseph Summers thought the plane near perfect, declaring upon landing: "I don't want anything touched." But six months later, the RAF took over the prototype for handling trials and found the plane lacking in some respects. It floated on landing as if it could not bear to return to earth, and the canopy was hard to open in an emergency at speeds greater than 300 miles per hour. But the Air Ministry was sufficiently taken with the Spitfire to order 310, confident that the fighter's shortcomings would soon be remedied.

And they were. The flaps were modified so the plane could settle to the ground faster in a landing. The canopy was redesigned with a small panel that the pilot could dislodge with his elbow, equalizing the air pressure inside and outside the cockpit so that the canopy could be opened at high speeds. Other minor changes were made, but regrettably, Reginald Mitchell was not present to see them incorporated into his fighter. He was suffering from cancer and died of the disease in June 1937. The first Spits were delivered to the RAF in mid-1938.

An airplane never looks finished to its creator. "The designer does not only see the aircraft that is flying today," Willy Messerschmitt once said. "No, he looks much further into the future. Long before an aircraft is finished, he knows how it could have been improved. Our work will never cease." And so it was, not just with his Me 109 but with the Spitfire as well. By the summer of 1940, when the fighters met in the Battle of Britain, both had undergone modifications in airframe and engine.

The Me 109 got a 1,100-horsepower Daimler-Benz engine, a new radiator cowling, and smoother joints between wing and fuselage to increase the plane's speed. The Spitfire was similarly but more extensively modified. It gained half a mile per hour when a flexible radio antenna that bent to the slip stream replaced its rigid one. Another nine miles per hour were added by setting rivets flush with the aluminum skin and polishing the wings and fuselage. Other adjustments—a retractable tail wheel and a curved windscreen, for example—helped add more than 10 per cent to the Spitfire's top speed of 350 miles per hour.

But even more important were the increases in power wrung from the Merlin by Rolls-Royce. The engine in the Spitfire prototype produced 990 horsepower. By the time the Battle of Britain began four years later, the Merlin could churn out 1,310 horsepower, a 32 per cent increase and 210 horsepower more than provided by the Me 109's Daimler-Benz. Some of this boost came from the simple step of directing the Merlin's exhaust, which roared from the engine at about 1,300 miles per hour, toward the rear of the plane, helping thrust it forward. The Merlin gave Mitchell's fighter an edge over the Me 109 in the Battle of Britain. The Spitfire stripped German bomber formations of fighter protection and left them vulnerable to the slower but no less lethal Hurricanes.

In the autumn of 1941, after Britain had gone on the offensive with bomber raids across the Channel, a new menace appeared in the skies. On September 21, 1941, a squadron of Spits reported shooting down "one unknown enemy aircraft with a radial engine." The plane was the Focke-Wulf Fw 190, a new and potent fighter.

The Fw 190 was the work of Kurt Tank. The indefatigable Tank had gotten his start in aviation in 1924, at a company named Rohrbach Metal Airplane Builders. He arrived there with a degree in electrical engineering—to his disappointment, the school he attended did not offer one in aeronautics—and he was put to work redesigning the hull of a flying boat the company had built.

Success in that assignment led to others and Tank's reputation at Rohrbach grew. But the company was committed to building flying boats, a type that Tank rightly saw as a dinosaur plodding toward extinction. So he left Rohrbach for BFW, where he worked under Messerschmitt. Tank soon formed the opinion that Messerschmitt, in his eagerness to save weight in his airframes, sacrificed too much in strength and safety. Tank left BFW after 18 months and signed on in the autumn of 1931 as chief of design with the Focke-Wulf company.

At that time, the firm built small, open-cockpit biplanes that were suitable, in Tank's view, only for weekend flying. Tank muffed his first chance to change the direction of the company when his entry in the Air Ministry's 1935 fighter competition, the Fw 159, lost out to the Me 109.

But in 1936 he got another chance. Tank proposed a spectacular new

To meet the threat of the German Focke-Wulf 190 in dogfights, the RAF modified the original, elliptical-wing Spitfire (right). The new Spitfire Mark XII (below) had a more powerful engine, a larger rudder and a clipped wing to improve performance between 5,000 and 18,000 feet.

transport that would outperform Germany's best airliner, the three-engined Junkers Ju 52. Tank's plane would have four engines so that it could continue flying even if two failed. To reduce drag and maximize lift, it would have long, narrow wings, and both fuselage and wings would be covered with a smooth aluminum skin instead of the corrugated skin of the Ju 52. It would carry up to 30 passengers, and cruise 60 miles per hour faster than the Junkers, with 60 per cent greater fuel efficiency. Tank would call his plane the Condor.

Tank showed the design to Baron von Gablenz, Deutsche Lufthansa's director. Von Gablenz was intrigued and asked Focke-Wulf to build a mock-up of the plane. Design details were worked out, and in mid-summer the airline ordered a prototype. Von Gablenz asked whether Tank could have the plane ready in two years.

"Oh, no," Tank answered. "You don't know our Bremen works if you say that."

"Three years, then?" asked the baron.

"I shall have your first Condor ready to take off in 12 months' time. And what's more, I'll bet a case of champagne on it." Tank lost the bet—by 11 days—so he dutifully packed off a case to the baron. A few days later, he received a similar shipment from von Gablenz. In the Lufthansa director's opinion, Tank had won the bet, in spirit if not in fact.

The Condor would succeed admirably as a transport, but with the outbreak of the War, the plane would enter service as a maritime patrol bomber. The Condor's depredations against Allied shipping were such that Winston Churchill would refer to the plane as "the scourge of the Atlantic." Only the eventual deployment of small aircraft carriers as convoy escorts would bring the Condor menace under control.

As the first of the Condors neared completion, the Air Ministry came to Focke-Wulf with a new assignment for Tank: to design a fighter to supplement the Me 109. It was a tribute to Tank's genius that he was the only designer solicited for the project.

Tank, perhaps unjustly, regarded the Me 109 and the Spitfire as race horses of a sort, too highly bred, too temperamental and too fragile for the work of war. He envisioned his fighter, the Fw 190, as a cavalry charger, fast but heavier and sturdier than those thoroughbreds. However, the designer's goal might have been unattainable if not for a new engine then undergoing tests at Bayerische Motoren Werke (BMW). Designated the BMW 139, it was a 14-cylinder, air-cooled radial capable of putting out a prodigious 1,550 horsepower.

"The design of the Fw 190," recalled Tank after the War, "was very much a team effort. I dare say a really good designer could have produced such a fighter all by himself, but it would have taken about eight years and at the end of that time nobody would have been the least bit interested in it." A year after the Air Ministry knocked on Focke-Wulf's door, the Fw 190, 29 feet long with wings spanning 31 feet, was ready for its first test flight. At 7,000 pounds, it weighed more than twice as much as the Me 109, a clear sign of the strength built into it;

Focke-Wulf technical director and chief designer Kurt Tank (right) points proudly to kills scored by a Luftwaffe pilot flying the Fw 190. Unlike most other German designers, Tank personally flight-tested every airplane he designed.

A Luftwaffe Focke-Wulf 190 fighter passes low over a European harbor in 1942. The design combined simple yet sturdy construction with outstanding performance; some 20,000 were mass-produced during the War in more than a dozen versions.

the wheels were widely spaced for excellent handling on the ground.

The job of piloting the plane fell to Hans Sander, a young aeronautical engineer and Focke-Wulf test pilot. On June 1, 1939, Sander took off in the plane. "Once airborne," he said, "I spiraled up to about 6,000 feet, keeping close overhead the airfield so that those on the ground could see what was happening." Twenty minutes later, after simulating a landing approach in midair to get the feel of the plane at low speeds, Sander "extended the flaps and undercarriage, and made a perfectly ordinary landing. There was no drama of any sort—drama is the last thing a test pilot wants with a new aircraft."

To Tank, Sander reported that "the controls were light and well-balanced, and the aircraft had not demonstrated any vices." Well, perhaps just a few. A short time into the flight, he began to perspire. "The rear of the engine was hard up against the front wall of the cockpit," he said later. "The temperature in the cockpit rose to 131° F.; I felt as though I was sitting with my feet in a fire." Then exhaust fumes began to seep into the cockpit, forcing Sander to don an oxygen mask.

Further tests revealed that the Fw 190 had another difficulty—one it shared with the early Spitfire. Air pressure made it impossible for the pilot to open the canopy when the plane was flying at high speed. To remedy the problem, a blank 20-millimeter cannon shell was rigged to blow the canopy off in an emergency. Improved seals around the cockpit kept out exhaust gases. A BMW 801 radial engine of 1,600 horsepower was installed slightly forward of the original engine's position, and the cockpit was shifted a few inches to the rear, pulling the pilot's feet out of the "fire." The wing was lengthened by three and a half feet to compensate for the extra weight of the new power plant.

When the Fw 190 first went into battle in mid-1941, it could outclimb the Spitfire and fly 10 miles per hour faster. The Spit could turn inside the Fw 190, but that was not enough to catch Tank's nimble fighter; with the 190's superior roll rate, a German pilot could snap his plane in the opposite direction, faster than a Spitfire could follow, and escape.

Tank's Butcherbird, as the Fw 190 was called by Focke-Wulf, alarmed RAF Fighter Command. "There is no doubt in my mind, nor in the minds of my fighter pilots," wrote Air Chief Marshal Sholto Douglas, 10 months after the German plane's combat debut, "that the Fw 190 is the best all-around fighter in the world today." The Butcherbird carried four machine guns and two 20-millimeter cannon, and already there were reports of more horsepower being harnessed to it.

The Fw 190 was a fine aircraft, but Douglas had overreacted. Rolls-Royce engineers soon substituted a new engine, the Griffon, for the Merlin. The Griffon produced 2,050 horsepower, enabling the Spitfire to compete successfully with the most advanced Fw 190s it faced.

But by now, aircraft designers recognized that prop-driven fighters would never fly much faster than the 450 miles per hour achieved by the Spitfire and the Fw 190. At higher speeds, the power necessary to overcome air resistance increased greatly. A larger, heavier engine would be needed, one that would demand more fuel. To accommodate the additional weight of metal and fuel, designers would have to create bigger, heavier planes, whose speed would not be much greater than that of the aircraft they replaced. And to complicate matters further, at speeds in excess of 450 miles per hour, the efficiency of propellers declined rapidly. Despite these obstacles, fighters continued to improve, culminating in the P-51H Mustang, with a top speed of 485 miles per hour. An experimental version of the Republic P-47 Thunderbolt, a long-range American fighter that entered the War in 1943, achieved a speed of 504 miles per hour in August 1944. But for all practical purposes, there seemed to be a 500-mile-per-hour speed limit on prop-driven aircraft. Fortunately, there was a new invention that promised to break this stalemate: the turbojet.

In its basic form, the jet engine seemed a veritable Buck Rogers kind of power plant. A rotating compressor—a wheel made up of numerous fan blades—sucked air into the front of the engine, compressed it, and expelled it into a combustion chamber where the air would be mixed with fuel and then ignited. The resulting hot gases spun a turbine wheel as they roared from the combustion chamber to propel the plane. The turbine wheel in turn drove the compressor, which sucked in more air, continuing the process. In contrast to a piston engine, a jet engine would run more efficiently the higher and faster a plane flew.

Two men deserve credit for inventing this extraordinary power plant: Frank Whittle in Great Britain and Hans von Ohain in Germany. Working independently of each other, they did more to advance aviation than any other individuals up to their time except the Wright brothers. Though the turbojet was simple enough in theory, it proved far

Blending British and American ingenuity

One of the finest fighters of World War II, the North American P-51 Mustang was designed almost by chance. In 1940, a British purchasing commission asked James "Dutch" Kindelberger, president of North American, to produce Curtiss P-40 fighters for the RAF. When Kindelberger proposed instead that his company build a completely new fighter that would be even better, the British accepted the offer—but stipulated that the prototype must be ready within 120 days.

North American beat the deadline by three days, and a year later the first Mustang arrived in England, to be followed by 300 others. At 382 mph, they proved faster than the latest Spitfire model, and their square-cut wings incorporated a special low-drag airfoil that helped give more difficult to create than either of its inventors initially realized.

Whittle was the first of the two to consider using the hot exhaust from a turbojet to power a plane. The idea occurred to Whittle, a 22-year-old graduate of the RAF's elite military academy, in 1929, when he was undergoing flight-instructor training. A French inventor had patented a device using the same principle in 1921, but nothing came of it. Up to Whittle's time gas turbines had been designed for industrial use. Even if shrunk to fit planes, they would have been far too heavy and inefficient to be practical—and most engineers thought they would remain so.

But not Whittle. He was certain that with careful attention to the design of the engine's various components, the jet could be made much lighter and more efficient. And so he set out on a quest that would cause some critics of his idea to regard him as deluded, even a bit mad. But Whittle also had supporters. His superiors at the flying school, for example, were so impressed with a design he had drawn up in his spare time that they arranged for him to show it to the Air Ministry. "The result," Whittle recalled, "was extremely disappointing. The net outcome was a letter from the ministry to the effect that any form of gas turbine was 'impracticable.'" A turbojet would be too heavy and burn too much fuel, the Ministry's experts said, to be suitable for aircraft.

Whittle thought they were wrong. In spite of criticism and his own occasional self-doubts, he pressed on. He patented his invention but, lacking funds to renew the patent, let it expire in 1935. At this critical

the Mustangs a range 60 per cent greater than the Spitfire's. Because their 1,100-hp Allison engines performed poorly at high altitudes, however, they were assigned only to low-level tactical reconnaissance and ground-attack missions.

The Americans, meanwhile, had taken relatively little notice of the Mustang. Then, in 1942, a U.S. military attaché in London suggested mating it to the superb Rolls-Royce engine that powered the Spitfire. The marriage worked: The re-engined Mustang flew 440 mph at 30,000 feet, with an 810-mile range.

Now the Allies at last possessed the long-range escort fighter they needed. Pressed into service by the USAAF as the P-51B, it could fly to the target using external fuel tanks, jettison them before combat, then fight and return home on its regular fuel supply. By the War's end, some 15,000 Mustangs had been built in seven major models.

Fitted with underwing drop tanks, the Mustang P-51D had a range of more than 2,000 miles.

juncture, a few of Whittle's close friends, former RAF officers who saw the potential in the jet engine, decided to seek financial support for his work. Eventually, they persuaded O. T. Falk and Partners, a small commercial banking firm, to lend funds with which to renew the patent and establish a firm, called Power Jets Ltd., that would build a demonstration engine. The Air Ministry stipulated that Whittle, who was still in the RAF, spend no more than six hours a week on the project. "This proviso," he recollected, "I ignored."

Whittle, who by this time had earned a degree in mechanical science from Cambridge, threw himself into the development of his Whittle Unit, or WU. Finally, on April 12, 1937, it stood bolted to a test-bed with its exhaust pipe poking out a window at the British Thomson-Houston Company, where the turbine and compressor had been made. Sheets of steel one inch thick surrounded the device to protect Whittle and a handful of assistants from flying parts if the WU disintegrated.

For the engine to start, it had to be turned at 1,000 revolutions per minute by an electric motor; that part of the test went smoothly. But when Whittle slowly opened the main fuel valve, "immediately, with a rising scream," as he put it, "the engine began to accelerate out of control. I promptly shut the valve, but the uncontrolled acceleration continued. Everyone around took to their heels except me. I was paralyzed with fright and remained rooted to the spot." To Whittle's relief, the engine slowed. The problem turned out to be a puddle of kerosene that had been deposited in the jet's combustion chamber during tests of the fuel pump. Once the puddle was consumed, the engine decelerated.

A drain installed in the combustion chamber cleared up the trouble. But the next day, the engine went out of control again, this time because a faulty valve let in too much fuel. "This experience," said Whittle, "was more frightening than the first because local overheating had caused combustion chamber joints to leak and the escaping fuel vapor took fire above the engine. Altogether a petrifying situation—except for those who once more disappeared with record-breaking speed." Clearly, Whittle had a lot of work to do on his WU.

Over the next two years, Whittle struggled with problems. The original engine became so worn that it had to be rebuilt. Then the engine lost several turbine blades. It was rebuilt again, yet it was still not right. Combustion chambers had to be redesigned, erratic fuel pressures stabilized. Fuel vaporizers failed to vaporize fuel. Bearings burned out. Each setback took weeks, or months, to overcome.

Three years later, Whittle was ready to show off the WU to the Air Ministry. On June 30, 1939, he ran it in a 20-minute demonstration for Dr. David R. Pye, Deputy Director of Scientific Research for the Air Ministry. By now, British officialdom had begun to show casual interest in the engine—government money had helped pay for rebuilding the WU twice and for some of the experimentation necessary to perfect it. This demonstration turned Pye into an enthusiast. Within weeks, Power Jets was awarded a contract to develop an engine suitable for an experi-

Pioneers of the turbojet era

A British laborer, pouring concrete for a landing strip one day in 1941, paused in his work and looked across the airfield. "I saw an airplane come out from the hangars," he recalled, "with no propeller! That fascinated me more than anything, as we were used to seeing airplanes with propellers. It took off, circled 'round, whistlin', and disappeared into the clouds."

The man had witnessed the takeoff of the revolutionary Gloster E.28/39, Britain's first jet-propelled aircraft. Nearly two years earlier, in Europe, Germany had flown a jet of its own, the Heinkel He 178. Developed independently, both aircraft proved that their turbojet engines were a practical means of propulsion.

The planes are shown here in scale, as are their engines on the next two pages.

HEINKEL HE 178 (1939)

GLOSTER E.28/39 (1941)

Germany's Heinkel S-3B

Heinkel's S-3B engine *(below)*, created by Hans von Ohain, and the Gloster's W.1 *(right)*, designed by Frank Whittle, established the formula for jet power: Air sucked into the engine is used to burn fuel in combustion chambers, and the exhaust is expelled to produce thrust.

In the S-3B, incoming air was accelerated by a two-stage compressor, then directed through ducts toward spray bars that injected fuel. After the mix was ignited by a spark plug *(not visible)*, the resulting hot gases rushed past the stator—stationary blades that directed the exhaust out of the single, ring-shaped combustion chamber. The exhaust then turned a turbine that drove the compressor, mounted on the same shaft.

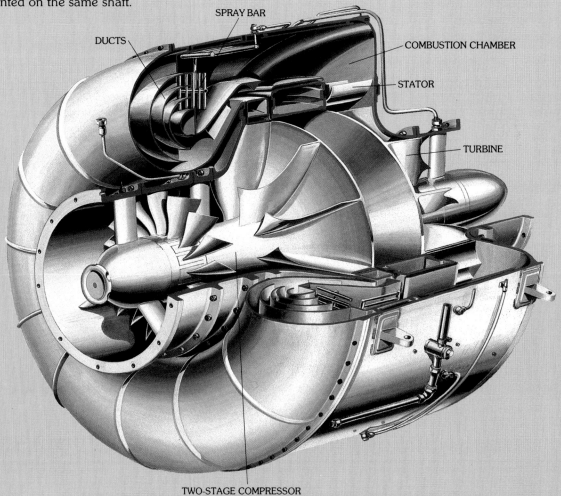

SPRAY BAR

DUCTS

COMBUSTION CHAMBER

STATOR

TURBINE

TWO-STAGE COMPRESSOR

Britain's Whittle W. 1

Air passed into the W.1 through ducts in the engine's front cover. After being accelerated by the compressor, it flowed through air guides into feed pipes to the engine's 10 combustion chambers.

Reversing direction as it rushed into the combustion chambers from the rear, the air swirled past spray vanes for its charge of fuel. Then the mixture was ignited by spark plugs, as in the S-3B. Air from pipes projecting into the combustion chambers swirled the blazing mixture to assure thorough burning of the fuel before the exhaust was piped to a stator and the engine's turbine.

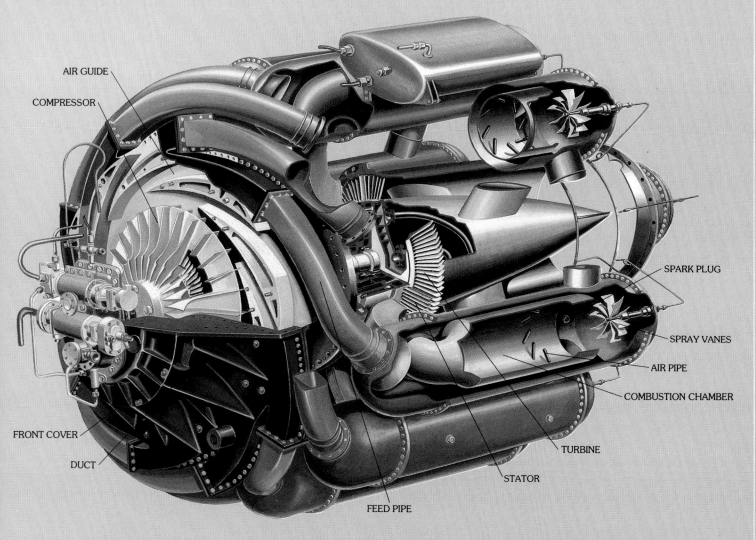

AIR GUIDE

COMPRESSOR

SPARK PLUG

SPRAY VANES

AIR PIPE

COMBUSTION CHAMBER

FRONT COVER

DUCT

TURBINE

STATOR

FEED PIPE

mental aircraft, to be built by the Gloster Aircraft Company. Indeed, Air Ministry officials became so convinced of the turbojet's potential that, before work on it was completed, they assigned Gloster the job of designing a twin-engined jet fighter, the Meteor.

By this time, however, the British no longer enjoyed a monopoly on turbojet technology. Unknown to them, the Germans, with whom Great Britain was already at war, had leaped ahead.

In February 1937, about two months before Whittle's WU ran out of control, Hans von Ohain, a young and brilliant engineer, fired up a demonstration engine of his own. Unlike Whittle's jet, Ohain's burned hydrogen—and it functioned just as he had predicted it would. It accelerated uneventfully to full speed, then slowed obediently when the fuel was cut off. "The apparatus," Ohain recalled, "fully met expectations."

A major factor in Ohain's success was that he worked for Ernst Heinkel. Right out of engineering school, Ohain had brought his idea for a jet engine to Heinkel. Despite the reservations expressed by his engineers, Heinkel had seized on Ohain's proposal, seeing it as a way to enter the aircraft-engine business at a time when there seemed to be little need for more manufacturers of piston engines in Germany. He had provided everything the inventor needed, though he was by no means certain at first that the idea was a practical one. The successful test run had a positive effect. "Heinkel and his engineers," commented Ohain later, "suddenly believed firmly in the feasibility of turbojet propulsion."

Heinkel instructed Ohain to convert his hydrogen-powered model into an engine that would burn kerosene and produce enough thrust— 1,100 pounds—to power a small experimental aircraft, to be called the He 178. Design of the airframe was assigned to the brothers Walter and Siegfried Günter, the Heinkel Company's two most innovative engineers. The goal was to finish the plane by mid-1939.

On August 27 of that year, everything was ready. As Heinkel, his technical staff and the riggers who had assembled the plane watched, company test pilot Erich Warsitz climbed into the cockpit. The He 178 was a peculiar-looking aircraft with an air inlet in the nose, where an engine and propeller might be expected. It had tapered wings 24 feet long, mounted just below the top of the 25-foot fuselage, and a conventional landing gear with a retractable tail wheel and main gear. Warsitz taxied the plane to the end of the runway, accelerated and took off. "He was flying!" Heinkel later recalled. "A new era had begun. The hideous wail of the engine was music to our ears. He circled again, smoothly and gracefully. The riggers began to wave like madmen. Calmly he flew around once more, and when six minutes were up he started to land. He cut out the jet unit, then misjudged his approach and had to sideslip. Sideslip with a new, dangerous, and tricky plane! We held our breath, but the He 178 landed perfectly, taxied and came to a stop— a magnificent landing. Within seconds we had all rushed over to Warsitz and the plane. The riggers hoisted both of us onto their shoulders and

An unpainted Messerschmitt 262, captured in Germany and brought to the United States for testing, still bears its Luftwaffe markings. Flown by Army Air Forces pilots, the jet was found to be superior to any Allied fighter of the War.

carried us round, roaring with enthusiasm. The jet plane had flown.''

Heinkel, however, did not have the monopoly on the turbojet that he had hoped for. In the few years since he had hired Ohain, the Air Ministry had engaged three mainstays of the country's aircraft-engine industry—BMW, Junkers, and Brandenburg Motor Works (Bramo)— to develop jet engines of their own. By the time the He 178 took to the air, these companies were well on the way to having engines with more power and greater fuel economy and reliability than Heinkel's.

Shortly after the He 178's first flight, the Air Ministry asked Heinkel to design a fighter, to be called the He 280 and powered by one or another of these companies' engines. At the same time the Ministry gave a similar commission to his archrival, Willy Messerschmitt, for a plane designated the Me 262. Heinkel's twin-engined prototype, the He 280, was ready first in September 1940, but BMW, Junkers and Bramo had yet to produce an engine. Heinkel plunged ahead anyway, installing power plants of his own manufacture.

The He 280 proved to be a remarkably capable and advanced aircraft. Though the engines were not yet producing the 1,600 pounds of thrust expected of them, the He 280 reached a top speed of 485 miles per hour on an early test flight. It boasted a number of innovations. It had the world's first ejection seat, which blasted the pilot clear of the plane with a charge of compressed air. It also had a tricycle landing gear, with a retractable nose wheel instead of a tail wheel; this allowed it to sit level on the ground. In mock combat it far outflew the Fw 190, Germany's best piston-engined fighter. Heinkel expected a prompt Luftwaffe commission for full-scale production. He was to be disappointed.

Messerschmitt's Me 262 was at last ready. It was the work of a design team headed by Woldemar Voigt, a protégé of Messerschmitt who was little known outside the firm. From his crew of 175 engineers, Voigt had chosen about 50 of the most imaginative for an advanced-design group; the rest translated their colleagues' ideas into production drawings.

Voigt encouraged the advanced group to seek the best solutions to the unusual problems facing them. Cost was no object, yet the plane had to be simple to produce; Germany was suffering from a severe shortage of skilled workers, especially toolmakers. To reward his designers for ideas approved for production, Voigt raised their salaries.

BMW seemed close to completing a workable engine of 1,500 pounds thrust, but that would not be enough to push the Me 262 past 500 miles per hour. So Voigt settled on two engines, even though they would produce much more thrust than required. The extra power could be used to advantage—the jet could now carry more fuel and heavier armament. Tankage for 476 gallons, plus a reserve of 53 gallons, was built into the fuselage, enabling the Me 262 to stay in the air for up to an hour. And four 30-millimeter cannon in the nose gave it a more potent arsenal than the three 20-millimeter cannon proposed for the He 280.

The Me 262's engines were to have been installed in the wings, as in a prop-driven plane. But Voigt's designers soon realized that it would be better to hang the engines below the wings, where they would not disturb the smooth flow of air over the airfoil.

The Me 262's fuselage acquired a distinctive shape as work progressed—wider at the bottom, when viewed head on, than at the top. This sharklike cross section was contributed by Ludwig Bölkow, of the advanced design team, after it became obvious that the wings, made thin to reduce drag, had space for retracting the undercarriage struts but not the wheels. Bölkow proposed widening the fuselage at the bottom to house the wheels when the struts folded into the wings. The landing gear's third wheel was placed in the usual location, under the tail.

By early 1941 the new plane was ready, but the BMW engines were not. Messerschmitt had to wait until November for them. Then, on the first takeoff, blades in the compressors failed, and both engines flamed out. Fortunately, a piston engine had been installed in the Me 262 while the jets were being readied. Because of the propeller, Messerschmitt's chief test pilot, Fritz Wendel, was able to land the plane in one piece.

Abandoning BMW, Messerschmitt turned to a more promising turbine, the Jumo 004, being perfected at Junkers by the company's designer, Anselm Franz. The Jumos were bigger and heavier than the BMWs, requiring further adjustments in the Me 262's design. The wings were angled back to balance the added weight.

Howard Hughes's Spruce Goose

In the summer of 1942, with German U-boats wreaking havoc on Allied shipping, industrialist Henry J. Kaiser proposed construction of "an aerial freighter beyond anything Jules Verne could have imagined." Joining forces with Howard Hughes, the eccentric but brilliant pilot and innovator, Kaiser won a government contract for a fleet of giant flying boats. It was Hughes's job to see the project to completion.

The contract stipulated that the planes be built of nonstrategic materials—in this case, wood. Construction of the prototype began in a specially erected 10-story building in Culver City, California, where workers glued, shaped and molded the components for the world's largest airplane. Though birch was used, the Hughes-Kaiser HK-1, as it was designated, was soon being referred to as the Spruce Goose.

The War ended and the contract expired before the prototype was done, but Hughes doggedly continued the project with his own money. At last, on June 11, 1946, the completed sections were moved to Long Beach Harbor for assembly. The finished eight-engined craft was a true leviathan—79 feet high and 218 feet long with a 320-foot wingspan.

On November 2, 1947, Hughes gingerly nosed the $28 million plane into the air for a brief flight only 70 feet above the harbor. But by then the era of flying boats was over, and the Spruce Goose was grounded forever. Nearly 35 years later, it was towed across the harbor to become a museum.

House movers slowly ease the hull of the Spruce Goose along the 28-mile route from Culver City to Long Beach (top right). Nearly 100,000 people lined the way to watch the six-day move. Overhead, cameramen—riding in a blimp owned by Hughes—photographed the scene (right).

The hull and wings of the Spruce Goose await assembly at Long Beach's Terminal Island. It took workmen 15 months to piece the aircraft's sections together and install the engines and the electrical, hydraulic and control systems.

Just before launching, the giant plane sits concealed under a huge tent Hughes ordered rigged out of canvas and metal pipes to protect it from the elements.

Inside the plane's cavernous hull, Hughes—wearing a fedora—checks the radio with operator Shell Bowen. The plane could carry a 130,000-pound payload.

Piloted by Hughes, the Spruce Goose takes off on what was supposed to be only a taxi run. "It felt so buoyant and good, I just pulled it up," said Hughes. The plane flew about a mile on its first and final voyage.

On July 18, 1942, the redesigned prototype was ready for testing, without the piston engine. But now Wendel found that the jet exhausts, angled downward because of the tail wheel, bounced off the runway and disrupted the flow of air over the tail. On the takeoff run, he had to tap the brakes to buck the tail into the air. Had he applied the brakes too hard, the Me 262 could easily have flipped over, killing him.

In the fifth prototype, the tail wheel was replaced by a nose wheel, which eliminated the need to apply the brakes on takeoff. The plane still had other shortcomings, however. Putting it into a steep bank created severe turbulence over the center of the wing, reducing lift. So the shape of the wing was refined even further, to smooth the airflow. The engines demanded gentle use of the throttles, since overeager handling might cause the jets to flame out or, worse, to catch fire from an excessive flow of fuel. Vibration in the turbines at certain throttle settings caused premature engine failure. To correct this problem, the Junkers company hired a professional violinist. With the engine off, he "played" the individual turbine blades with his bow to determine their natural frequency. The blades, it turned out, resonated at the operating speed of the engine, a coincidence that amplified small vibrations enough to fracture the blades. Franz's remedy was to taper the blades slightly to increase their natural frequency, and to cut the engine's operating speed from 9,000 to 8,700 revolutions per minute. The vibrations ceased.

Even with such growing pains, the Me 262 outshined the He 280, which carried less fuel and, though faster, suffered from severe tail vibrations—known as flutter—at high speed. Accordingly, the Luftwaffe chose the Me 262, taking delivery of its first battle-ready jets in June 1944; by the first of November, there were 315 of them in service.

The plane was a triumph. It was easier to fly than the Me 109, and it took less than 10 minutes from takeoff to climb above an Allied bomber group. Although it could not turn as tightly as the piston-engined fighters that defended the bombers, it could outrun them with a speed in excess of 550 miles per hour. Moreover, it could flash through a bomber formation so quickly that gunners inside the huge planes barely had time to draw a bead on the jet before it was out of range.

Neither Great Britain nor the United States had a fighter that could touch it. The Meteor, which joined RAF squadrons in small numbers a few months after the Messerschmitt joined the Luftwaffe, could not match the German jet's performance, and its range was too short for escorting bombers into Germany. The U.S. was even further behind. Its first operational jet fighter, Lockheed's Shooting Star, would not reach the U.S. Army Air Forces in operational quantities until after the War.

The advent of the turbojet was a watershed in the history of aviation. Before its appearance, aircraft could not maintain a speed of 500 miles per hour in level flight. The Me 262 smashed through that barrier as if it had never existed. But beyond lay another, one that would tax the imagination of designers and the courage of test pilots in the first decade after the War. They called it the sound barrier. ⌁

The airplane distilled to its essence

In 1923, aircraft designer Jack Northrop built a balsa model of a futuristic plane so streamlined it was practically all wing. That model was the first step toward realizing his dream of a flying wing.

Northrop believed that a pure wing—with no tail or fuselage to produce drag—could carry any load faster, farther and more economically than a conventional plane of similar size. And he envisioned the skies filled one day with his planes. Over the next three decades, Northrop doggedly built a series of such aircraft, ranging from the primitive 1929 flying wing *(page 95),* which retained a tail assembly, to the huge tailless YB-49 jet bomber *(left),* produced for the U.S. Army Air Forces.

The YB-49 was one of the fastest big planes of its day, with a speed of 500 mph, and in 1948 it set an endurance record by remaining aloft nine and a half hours without refueling. Nevertheless, a tight budget—and the fact that, among other things, the plane lacked the capacity to carry an atomic bomb—forced the Air Force to scrap the YB-49 in favor of the conventional B-36.

Exhaust smoke spewing from its eight turbojets, the 172-foot-wide YB-49— brainchild of designer Jack Northrop (above)—takes off from the Northrop Corporation's California field on its maiden flight, on October 21, 1947.

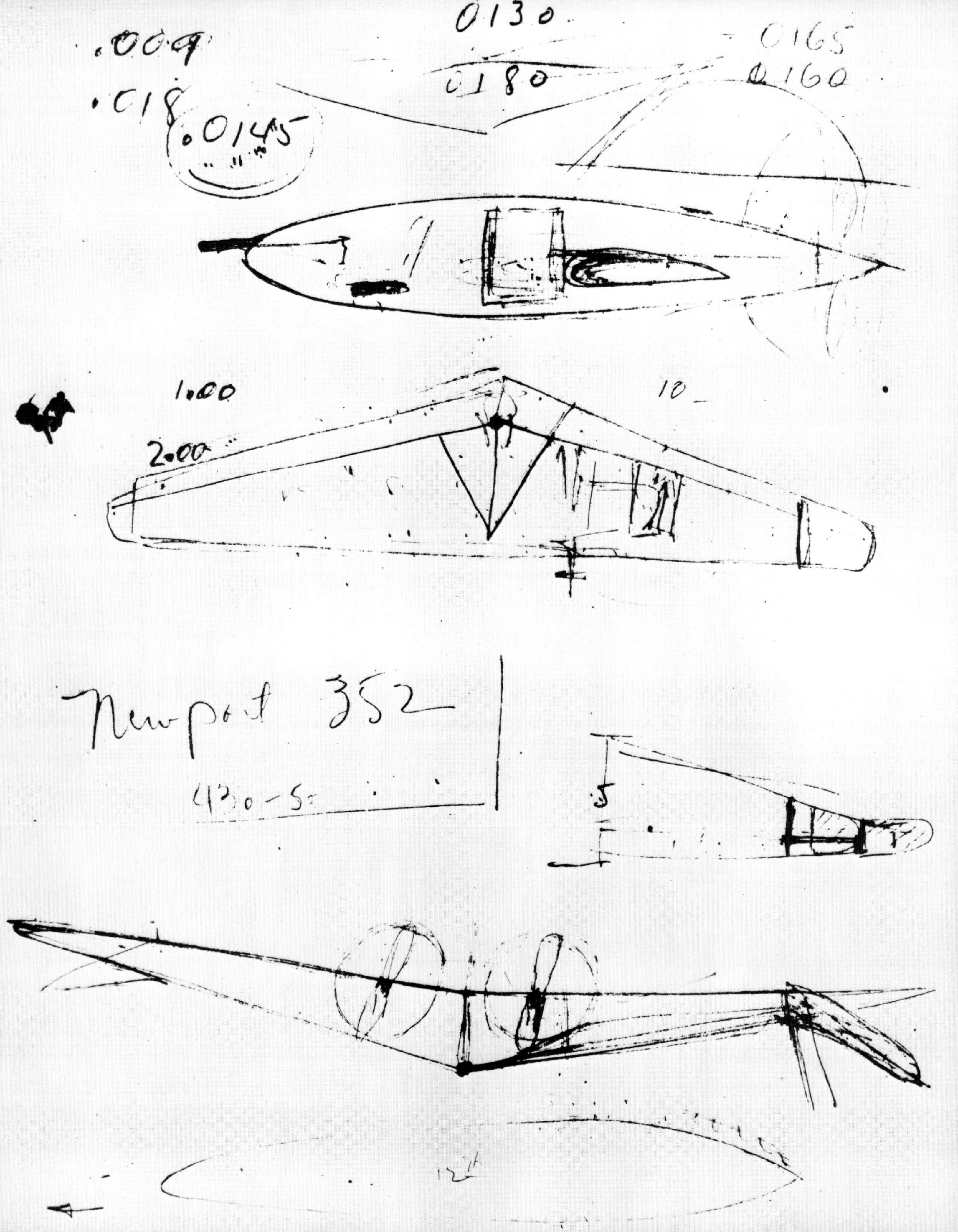

.009
.018
.0130
.0180
.0165
.0160
.0145

1.00
2.00
10

Newport 352
430-5
.5

An early model flying wing built in 1929 soars above the California countryside on its first flight. "We didn't dare go the whole way and eliminate the tail," said Northrop, who equipped the 30-foot-wide plane with tail surfaces on twin booms to insure against handling problems.

Workmen perform weight and balance tests on a more advanced flying wing built in 1940 and designated the N-1M. Flight tests revealed that the drooping wing tips were unnecessary, and the plane was rebuilt with straight wings.

A pilot puts the redesigned wing, designated the N-9M, through its paces on a 1942 flight. The 60-foot plane was a scale model of the XB-35 bomber (overleaf), which would be nearly three times as large. Pitch and roll were controlled by elevons, which combined the functions of elevator and aileron.

Photographed before its 1945 maiden flight, the XP-79B, a fighter derivative of the flying wing, features reinforced leading edges for ramming the tails of enemy planes. The jet crashed the first time up, killing its pilot.

Northrop's rough sketches of a flying wing (left), made during a 1939 meeting with a team of designers, show his concern with the plane's stability. The wing tips were to be slanted downward to give the tailless craft the best performance in flight.

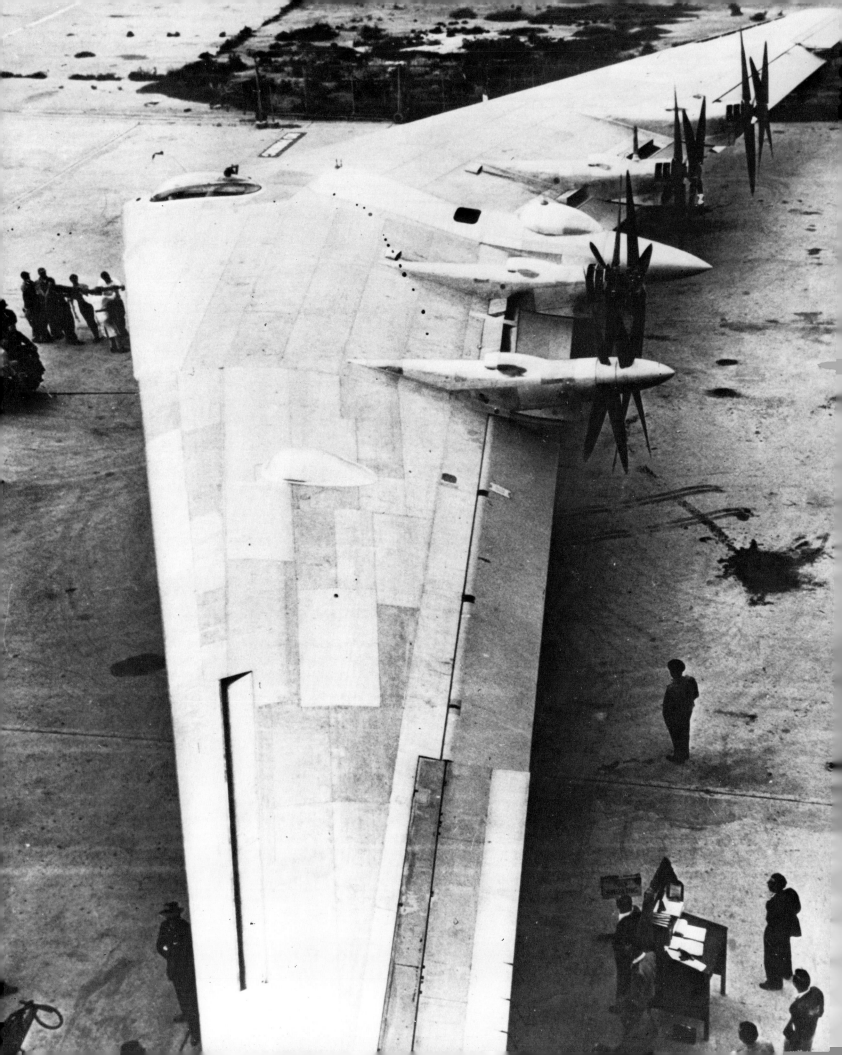

Northrop's XB-35 (above), the first full-scale bomber prototype, knifes through the sky during its first test flight, on June 15, 1946. To monitor performance, engineers installed a television camera that relayed pictures of the XB-35's instrument readings to a screen on board a P-61 chase plane, whose propeller spinner cap is visible at right.

Test pilot Max Stanley (left) and his crewmen accept congratulations after the XB-35's successful flight. The flying wing handled so well that Stanley was prompted to say: "I'd never have known the plane didn't have a tail if I didn't look behind me."

Bystanders examine the XB-35 on the Northrop runway (left). This plane and a second prototype were equipped with eight-blade, counter-rotating propellers, but gearbox problems developed and all models were eventually fitted with single four-blade props.

A mock-up of a passenger version of the
flying wing shows the luxury that "the airliner
of tomorrow" was to have offered. Plans
allowed room for 80 passengers.

A model gazes out the glassed-in leading
edge of the flying wing airliner mock-up. The
Northrop Corporation estimated that
the plane would "be capable of spanning
the United States in half-a-dozen hours."

Lined up like so many boomerangs at
the Northrop field, nine piston-engined
flying wings await the installation of
turbojets following successful tests of the
jet-powered YB-49. Only one plane
had been converted when the Air Force
abandoned the project in late 1949.

BLOHM UND VOSS BV 141B-0 (1938)
An observer, pilot and gunner occupied the BV 141's crew compartment. Offset to the right of the engine, the glassed-in nacelle countered the tendency of engine torque to roll a single-engined aircraft to the left. The horizontal stabilizer was mounted to one side to improve the gunner's field of fire. Mechanical problems caused the German Air Ministry to abandon the BV 141 in 1942.

Odd-looking warplanes that never saw combat

CHANCE VOUGHT V-173 (1942)

This pancake-shaped fighter prototype was built for the U.S. Navy. The nearly circular wing was to have permitted speeds as low as 20 mph for vertical takeoffs and landings from a ship steaming into the wind. The Navy dropped the project after tests revealed serious stability problems.

World War II yielded a collection of unusual airplanes on both sides of the conflict. Not one of these improbable birds was ever mass-produced, but they all flew. And some of the planes pioneered concepts, such as swept wings and tricycle landing gear, that later became standard features on high-performance aircraft.

Without exception, stringent military requirements inspired these airplanes. Germany's asymmetrical Blohm und Voss BV 141 *(above)* was a logical, if bizarre, solution to the problem of providing maximum visibility from a single-engined observation plane. The Chance Vought V-173 "Flying Flapjack" *(left)* resulted from the U.S. Navy's demand for a short-takeoff-and-landing (STOL) carrier fighter. Because the aeronautical oddities shown here and on the following pages did not work very well, all were scrapped during testing or shortly thereafter. The date each plane first flew is noted in parentheses, and the aircraft on adjacent pages are in scale.

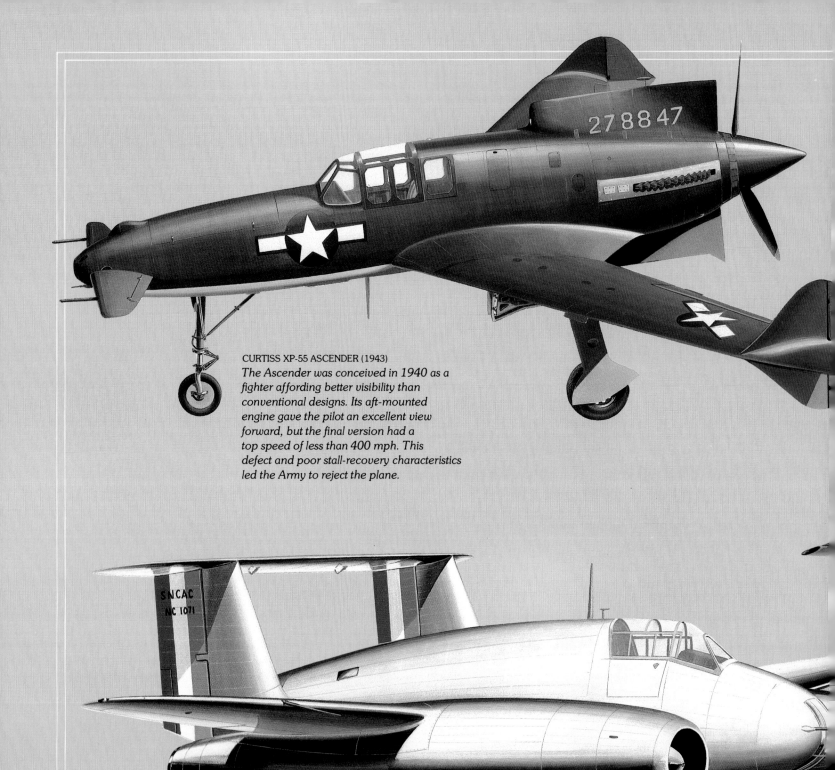

CURTISS XP-55 ASCENDER (1943)
The Ascender was conceived in 1940 as a fighter affording better visibility than conventional designs. Its aft-mounted engine gave the pilot an excellent view forward, but the final version had a top speed of less than 400 mph. This defect and poor stall-recovery characteristics led the Army to reject the plane.

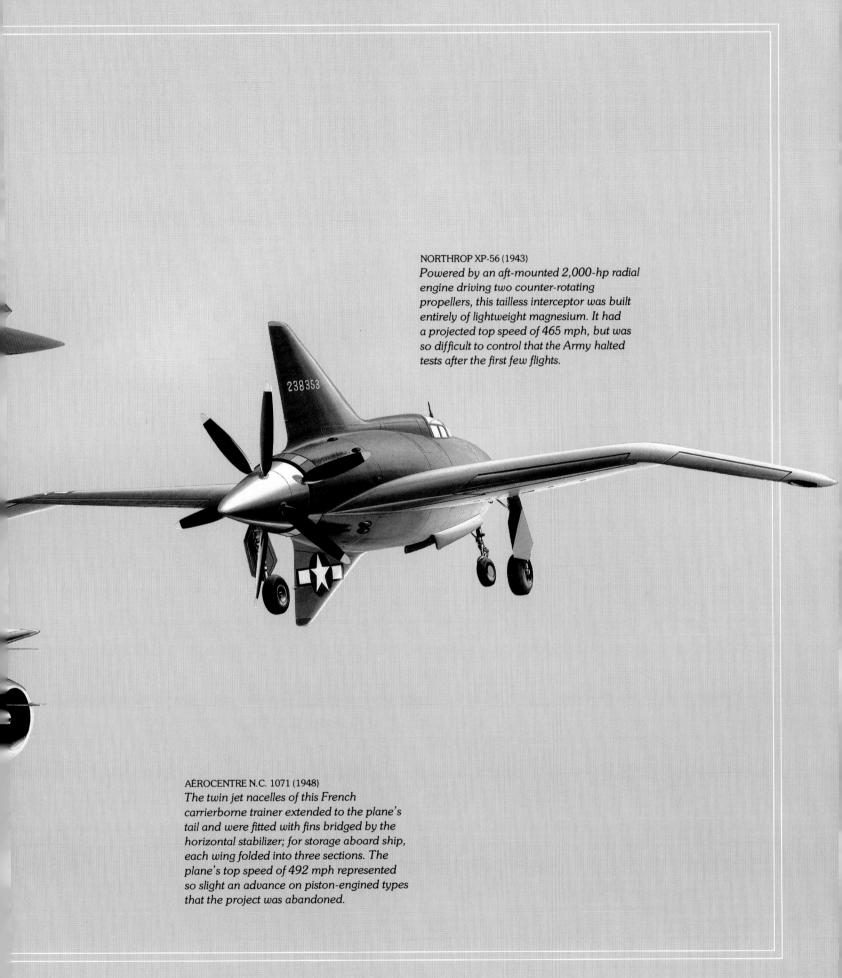

NORTHROP XP-56 (1943)
Powered by an aft-mounted 2,000-hp radial engine driving two counter-rotating propellers, this tailless interceptor was built entirely of lightweight magnesium. It had a projected top speed of 465 mph, but was so difficult to control that the Army halted tests after the first few flights.

AÉROCENTRE N.C. 1071 (1948)
The twin jet nacelles of this French carrierborne trainer extended to the plane's tail and were fitted with fins bridged by the horizontal stabilizer; for storage aboard ship, each wing folded into three sections. The plane's top speed of 492 mph represented so slight an advance on piston-engined types that the project was abandoned.

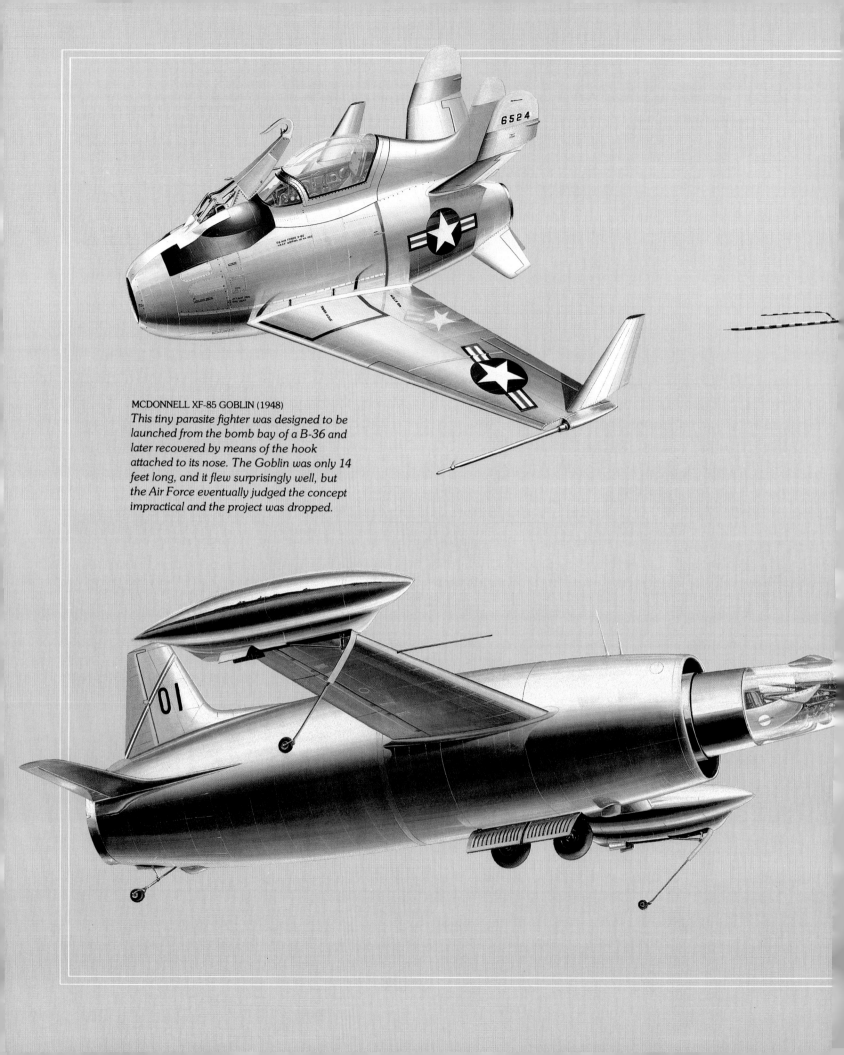

MCDONNELL XF-85 GOBLIN (1948)
This tiny parasite fighter was designed to be
launched from the bomb bay of a B-36 and
later recovered by means of the hook
attached to its nose. The Goblin was only 14
feet long, and it flew surprisingly well, but
the Air Force eventually judged the concept
impractical and the project was dropped.

REPUBLIC XF-91 (1949)
The wings of this experimental interceptor were inversely tapered—wider and thicker at the tips than at the roots—for better low-speed handling. A rocket beneath the butterfly tail, which had no vertical fin, supplemented the XF-91's jets. But the plane was only a slight improvement on other jet designs and never entered production.

LEDUC 010 (1947)
Powered by a ramjet, in which air for combustion is compressed solely by the plane's movement through the atmosphere, this French research craft had to be launched at high speed from a mother ship. An inner fuselage housed the cockpit and an outer shell framed the jet's circular air intake. Technically, the idea was sound, but the ramjet used too much fuel to be practical.

4

Rocketing past Mach 1

One morning in 1941, Lockheed test pilot Ralph Virden took off from the company's Burbank production plant in a P-38 Lightning, a fast, twin-engined interceptor. In a dive, the P-38 could achieve very high speeds, well over 500 miles per hour. But reports from Army pilots strongly suggested that all was not well with the P-38 when pushed to this limit: Sometimes it would buffet and shake violently, the nose trying to tuck under as the plane accelerated. Only by hauling back on the control column with all his strength could the pilot pull out of the dive. In hope of eliminating this problem, Lockheed engineers had devised an improved control system that would allow the pilot to exert more force on the elevators. Virden was aloft to try it out.

He began with a series of dives, pulling out at 15,000 feet. So familiar were Lockheed's plant workers with the snarling whine of P-38s being tested, that they hardly noticed Virden's plane racing and diving overhead. But on one dive the P-38 captured all attention as it arrowed down with its engine screaming louder and louder. Horrified onlookers watched as the Lightning's horizontal stabilizer ripped off and the remainder of the stricken aircraft plunged to the ground. The pilot was killed instantly. Virden had become one of the first victims of a little understood and soon dreaded phenomenon that was to pose the greatest challenge to aviation since the Wright brothers took to the air.

After the accident, Lockheed and the National Advisory Committee for Aeronautics (NACA) moved swiftly to make the P-38 safe in a dive. They added two large speed brakes to the underside of the wings. When extended into the airstream, these kept the P-38 from accelerating to a speed that would tear it apart. So modified, the plane went on to long and illustrious service in every theater of the War. But the speed brakes were only a stopgap measure, not an answer to the problem of high-speed flight.

Aeronautical scientists had known for nearly a decade that shock

The Bell X-1, first plane to break the sound barrier, hangs suspended from a B-29 Superfortress as the bomber rises from Muroc Army Air Field, California, on December 9, 1946. After release, the rocket plane climbed to 25,000 feet, where the thin air would offer little resistance as the X-1 reached more than 900 mph.

waves begin to form in the air around any object traveling near the speed of sound *(below)*. But that speed is not a constant—at sea level it is about 760 miles per hour, while at 40,000 feet it drops to 660 miles per hour. To avoid ambiguity, scientists adopted the convention of the Mach number, named for Ernst Mach, the 19th Century Austrian physicist who had measured the speed of sound. A plane's Mach number is equivalent to its speed divided by the speed of sound at the plane's altitude. Thus an aircraft flying at the speed of sound is said to have a velocity of Mach 1, regardless of altitude. A cockpit instrument, called a Machmeter, measures air speed according to this equation.

Virden had been diving at approximately Mach .7 when his P-38's horizontal stabilizer tore loose. Shock waves do not form until Mach 1, yet they had caused the plane's destruction. The apparent contradiction is easily explained. The speed of the air flowing past a plane in flight is never uniform. If it were, the plane would not fly; a wing produces lift in part because air travels faster across the top surface than across the bottom *(page 20)*. In Virden's fatal dive, the speed of the air over the wing was perhaps 700 miles per hour or more, well above Mach 1 at altitude. The resulting shock waves caused turbulence in the wake of the wing so violent that it wrenched off the tail. Theoreticians thought that the effects of shock waves might be less severe on the far side of Mach 1, but many doubted whether a plane accelerating toward the speed of sound could survive long enough for them to find out. Some spoke darkly of a sound barrier that no aircraft could safely pass.

Two American theoreticians, working independently of each other, did not share this view. To Ezra Kotcher, a civilian working for the Army Air Forces, and John Stack of NACA, the sound barrier seemed no more than a challenging puzzle to solve. The two could not have been less alike. Kotcher was academic-looking and slight

How shock waves form at the speed of sound

As a plane flies through the air, its motion creates small disturbances, or pressure waves, that radiate out from its surfaces.

At subsonic speeds, the waves move ahead of as well as behind the plane *(first diagram, right)*. But at the speed of sound *(second diagram)*, the waves can no longer move ahead, since the plane is traveling along with them. Thus they build up into a shock wave, perpendicular to the line of flight, that may impair the function of a plane's control surfaces.

At supersonic speeds, the plane leaves its pressure waves behind *(third diagram)*, and the shock wave bends back to form a "shock cone." When this cone reaches the earth's surface, the sudden change in pressure causes a sonic boom.

of build; he would patiently and methodically analyze a complex problem and then advance a solution, often a radical one. Stack was a dynamo of energy whose frequent flashes of creative brilliance compensated for his stubbornness. Both shared a conviction that it was possible to design a plane that would power its way right through any so-called sound barrier.

Using a full-sized, piloted research plane would be risky, for the craft could not be tested beforehand in a wind tunnel, the traditional tool for aerodynamic research. The difficulty lay in the very shock waves that engineers wished to study. Whenever the velocity of the wind in a tunnel exceeded Mach .75, the lower limit of the mysterious transonic region near the sound barrier, the shock waves streaming from a model bounced unpredictably from the surrounding walls, making observations unreliable. Above Mach 1.25, the problem disappeared.

Kotcher knew from a 1930s Army lecture that artillery shells suffered no ill effects traveling faster than sound. It struck him that supersonic flight appeared so forbidding chiefly because it could not be studied in a wind tunnel. The sound barrier was, as he put it, ''a wind tunnel technique barrier.'' Aviation had a choice: It could wait for a transonic wind tunnel to be invented, or it could forge ahead, circumventing the wind tunnel entirely with manned supersonic airplanes. While Kotcher worked largely alone on the idea for such a plane, Stack assembled at NACA a small team of young engineers, who set out to examine possible shapes for a transonic aircraft and to foresee the problems it might encounter as it rushed toward the sound barrier. Like Kotcher, Stack was convinced that a test aircraft, despite the risk involved to its pilot, would yield much more reliable and meaningful information than could be obtained by the alternatives—firing off rocket-propelled models, or dropping streamlined shapes from high altitudes to study their behavior at high speed.

By 1943, the work of Kotcher and Stack had assumed more than

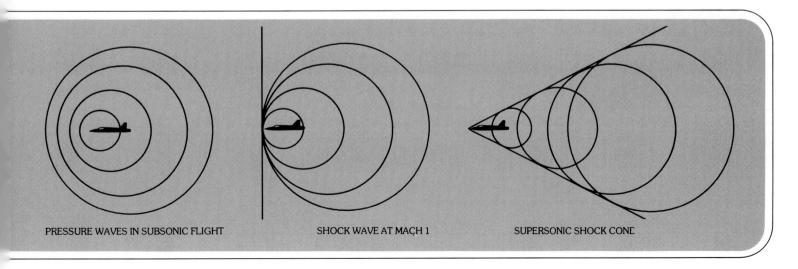

PRESSURE WAVES IN SUBSONIC FLIGHT   SHOCK WAVE AT MACH 1   SUPERSONIC SHOCK CONE

Hungarian-born Theodore von Kármán, whose research contributed greatly to the achievement of supersonic flight, makes an aerodynamic point on a blackboard. "High speed has its uses," he once said. "For me personally I prefer a slower pace. I like nothing better than to think of myself riding through Paris as my parents did in old Budapest—in a fiacre with a coachman and two horses."

academic interest. An epidemic of tail failures similar to the one that had killed Virden had spread among high-speed fighters, such as Britain's Hawker Typhoon. One day in 1942, for example, three Hawker Typhoons had dived on some Messerschmitt 109s over France; two of the RAF fighters crashed after their tails broke loose. Some designers sought to circumvent the problem by eliminating the tail from aircraft altogether; Jack Northrop's flying wings *(pages 92-99)* were one such attempt. In Germany, Alexander Lippisch was designing a tailless rocket interceptor, the Messerschmitt 163 Komet. But most engineers resorted to half measures—aerodynamic braking devices and tail surfaces constructed much more robustly than previously deemed necessary.

The assault on the sound barrier began to build momentum in 1944, after Ezra Kotcher published a paper comparing the merits of jet and rocket propulsion for a high-speed research aircraft. Kotcher's research, which he facetiously dubbed the "Mach 0.999 Study" because of the supposedly impenetrable sonic barrier, led him to recommend a rocket-powered craft. His calculations indicated that turbojets of the day could not achieve sufficient thrust to propel an airplane at supersonic speeds. Theodore von Kármán, director of the prestigious Guggenheim Aeronautical Laboratory at the California Institute of Technology and scientific consultant to the Army Air Forces, approved Kotcher's proposal, and by the fall of 1944 the AAF was eager to develop a rocket-propelled supersonic research airplane. John Stack at NACA was not so enthusiastic. He and a panel of agency engineers felt that a jet engine would be safer; rocket engines, with their explosive fuels, were relatively untried. But unlike the AAF, NACA lacked funds to commission a plane. So Stack and his colleagues went along with the military in its support of Kotcher's idea for a rocket-powered craft. All that was needed now was someone to design and build it.

On November 30, 1944, a well-known aircraft designer dropped by Ezra Kotcher's office at Wright Field for a chat. His name was Robert J. Woods, a 40-year-old graduate of the University of Michigan who, at the start of his aeronautical career at NACA's Langley Laboratory in 1928, had shared a desk with John Stack. Woods was a partner of Lawrence Dale Bell at the Bell Aircraft Corporation in Buffalo, New York. The name Bell was synonymous with innovative aircraft, and Woods, as chief engineer, had contributed to many of them. Together with Harlan Poyer, he developed a single-engined fighter in 1939 called the P-39 Airacobra. The engine was mounted behind the cockpit near the aircraft's center of gravity; power was transmitted to the propeller by a long shaft. Despite its imaginative design, the P-39 was underpowered, limiting its effectiveness as a fighter above 10,000 feet. Nonetheless, it saw extensive service with the Soviet Air Force under the Lend-Lease program.

Another of Woods's designs, the FM-1 Airacuda, was a twin-engined interceptor. It had pusher propellers, with a gunner seated in the front of each engine nacelle. The FM-1 might have proved useful, but its configuration was too radical for conventional-minded military planners. Then Woods directed the design effort that in 1942 produced the first U.S. jet airplane, the Bell XP-59A Airacomet.

Woods's visit to Wright Field was a stroke of luck. Kotcher had already spoken to other designers about a supersonic research airplane. While all agreed that such a vehicle would be valuable, the companies they worked for declined to undertake the project; the chance of being embarrassed by failure seemed too high. Woods and Bell Aircraft, Kotcher hoped, would be different.

Kotcher came directly to the point: Would Bell be interested in developing an airplane capable of attaining a speed of 800 miles per hour at 35,000 feet? Woods agreed on the spot. He called Larry Bell and said, "You'd better sit down and relax. I've got some news. I've just committed you to the production of an 800-mile-per-hour airplane." Bell was incredulous. "What have you done?" he groaned. But he had faith in his chief engineer and knew that Woods could deliver on his promises; he let the commitment stand. The AAF had found its contractor.

Woods returned immediately to Buffalo and picked a design team consisting of Robert Stanley, a Bell test pilot who had made the first flight in the XP-59A, and Bell's four ablest designers: Benson Hamlin, Paul Emmons, Stanley Smith and Roy Sandstrom. In December 1944, Bell, NACA and the AAF agreed on a payload: 500 pounds of instruments that would record the aerodynamic forces on the plane as it flew toward and, perhaps, through the sound barrier. Now the Bell team set to work in earnest.

Woods dispatched Ben Hamlin and Paul Emmons on a tour of the nation's aeronautical laboratories to gather what information they could on suitable configurations for this ambitious aircraft—what shape the fuselage should be, what kind of wings it should have, how the tail should be designed. "Various people told us the various thoughts that they might have," Hamlin later recalled, "but every single one of them also added in the same breath, 'We really can't tell you because we really don't know.'" In the end, the two engineers recommended that the plane's fuselage be modeled on the contours of a .50-caliber bullet, since ballistics experts agreed that the projectile's shape appeared to give it good stability at velocities approaching Mach 1.

There was substantial disagreement among the aerodynamicists over the wings: They should be thinner than conventional ones, but how much so? Engineers express the thickness of a wing as a percentage, actually the ratio of the wing's thickness to the distance between the leading and trailing edges, or chord. For most planes of the mid-1940s, the ratio ranged between 12 and 15 per cent. Some of the NACA staff advocated a 10 per cent wing for the X-1. An airfoil of that thickness would encounter the troublesome shock waves at a relatively low and safe speed. Others favored a wing of 8 per cent thickness to delay the onset of shock waves as long as possible. The aircraft would thus be exposed to them for a shorter time before escaping through the sound barrier. Bell's engineers deferred to Floyd Thompson, NACA's authority on wings. He examined evidence from both camps and concluded that a wing of 8 per cent thickness would be best for penetrating the sound barrier.

Then there was the tail to consider. John Stack recommended that Bell install the stabilizer on the fin, well above the turbulence that would form in the wing's wake at transonic speeds. Such turbulence could disrupt the smooth flow of air over the tail surfaces that was essential if a pilot was to retain control over the pitch of the aircraft. Stack also urged that the horizontal stabilizer be made thinner than the wing. Shock waves would then form on the wings at a lower speed than on the tail, making it unlikely that both would suffer ill effects simultaneously. Woods's group of engineers agreed, then went a step further. Suspecting from the behavior of airplanes in dives that elevators lost effectiveness at high speeds, they designed the entire horizontal stabilizer to pivot. Thus if the pilot needed more "control authority" near Mach 1 than afforded by the elevators, he could move the entire stabilizer with a trim switch mounted on the control column.

The plane would be small—31 feet long with a wingspan of 28 feet. For the cockpit, the designers devised a canopy that fit flush with the plane's nose; a protruding cockpit would have caused too much drag. The aircraft was required to withstand stresses at least twice the maximum anticipated by the AAF for its fighters. This seemed a formidable assignment, but as work on the plane progressed, Bell engineers discovered that to fulfill it demanded little more than thickening the aluminum skin of the wings to strengthen and stiffen them. Where the wings joined the fuselage, the skin was made a half inch thick; in a fighter, the skin at the same point measured $1/10$ inch thick.

The designers calculated that approximately 6,000 pounds of thrust would be required for four minutes to enable the plane to take off, climb to 35,000 feet and accelerate to 800 miles per hour. Fortunately there was a rocket engine suitable for the purpose, built by Aerojet Engineering Corporation of Pasadena, California. It had been intended for an experimental fighter called the XP-79, one of Northrop's flying-wing designs. As expected, the fuel for the plane's rocket engine posed acute safety problems. The Aerojet engine produced its 6,000 pounds of thrust by burning a mixture of two highly explosive liquids—red fuming nitric acid and aniline—in a single combustion chamber. So unstable were these compounds that when mixed, they ignited spontaneously.

To see firsthand what would happen when the chemicals were combined, members of the design team bought a bottle of each, taped them together and shattered them against some isolated rocks near the plant. The contents erupted in a fiery blast that left no doubt of the grave danger to the plane and pilot in the event of a fuel leak or takeoff accident.

Shaken by what they had seen, the Bell engineers turned to an engine produced by Reaction Motors, Inc. (RMI) of Pompton Plains, New Jersey. Actually four engines in one, this rocket burned a less dangerous mix of liquid oxygen (LOX) and diluted alcohol. Each combustion chamber produced 1,500 pounds of thrust; by firing them or shutting them down one at a time the pilot could regulate the power plant's output.

Bell's designers planned on using a new kind of high-speed fuel pump to feed the propellants into the RMI engine, but the pump was beset by problems. So they resorted to another fuel-delivery system, one employing nitrogen stored under high pressure in several steel spheres. As it turned out, the nitrogen tanks and associated plumbing added nearly a ton to the plane's weight, and because of the space the tanks occupied, they also cut the planned fuel load in half. In light of this, the engineers abandoned the idea of having the aircraft take off under its own power. Instead, a Boeing B-29 Superfortress would be modified to carry the rocket plane suspended from a shackle in the bomb bay and release it between 20,000 and 25,000 feet. When the rocket fuel was consumed, the craft would glide to earth for a dead-stick landing.

By May of 1945, the Bell team had all but completed the design. The AAF designated the plane the XS-1—Experimental Sonic-1—but the world would know it simply as the X-1. "It required an unhesi-

Anatomy of the X-1

This X-1, the second of three, has slightly thicker wings than the craft Chuck Yeager used to break the sound barrier in 1947.

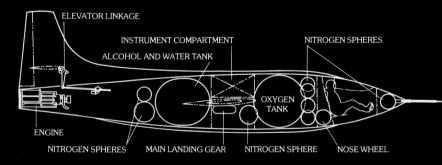

ELEVATOR LINKAGE

INSTRUMENT COMPARTMENT

NITROGEN SPHERES

ALCOHOL AND WATER TANK

OXYGEN TANK

ENGINE

NITROGEN SPHERES   MAIN LANDING GEAR   NITROGEN SPHERE   NOSE WHEEL

Two large spherical tanks hold the X-1's fuel, which was fed to the rocket engine by nonflammable nitrogen gas stored under pressure in smaller spheres. Nitrogen from the tank in the nose pressurized the cockpit.

The rocket engine in the X-1 had four combustion chambers, each producing 1,500 pounds of thrust. At full power, the rocket consumed its entire 4,680-pound fuel supply in just two and a half minutes.

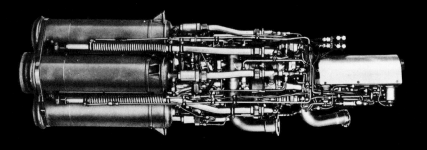

tating boldness to undertake a venture so few thought could succeed,'' one Bell engineer wrote later, ''an almost exuberant enthusiasm to carry across the many obstacles and unknowns, but most of all a completely unprejudiced imagination in departing so drastically from the known way.''

The AAF had ordered three X-1s. The first of them, with 8 per cent wings, emerged from a Bell assembly hangar in Buffalo two days after Christmas, 1945; the other two would not be ready for months. One would be flown by NACA pilots to make a detailed study of transonic flight; the last of the three, however, would be destroyed in an explosion on the ground before it could make a single powered flight. At this point, the X-1 had no engine; Reaction Motors had not yet finished work on the power plant. The aircraft would undergo its initial flights as a glider.

Trials began almost immediately. Buffalo in January was no place to test a new aircraft, so the flights were conducted in the balmy skies above Pinecastle Field, near Orlando, Florida. Bell test pilot Jack Woolams, a qualified engineer as were all the company's test pilots, was assigned to the trials.

On the 19th of January, a ground crew winched the X-1 into the bomb bay of the B-29 mother ship. The little plane, painted bright orange for high visibility, hung so low that it seemed in danger of scraping the runway as the B-29 took off. At an altitude of 5,000 feet, Woolams descended a short ladder from the bomb bay of the B-29 to a plywood platform hanging beneath the bomber, opposite the entry hatch of the X-1. Deafened by the noise of the B-29's engines and whipped by the plane's slip stream, in spite of walls built around the platform, Woolams wriggled feet first through the hatch and into the cockpit. He strapped himself in and secured the hatch. At 27,000 feet, with everything ready, the X-1 fell away from the bomber. It handled admirably during the 10-minute descent, and gliding tests continued.

By autumn, the X-1 had been approved for powered flight. The site chosen lay in the remote wastes of California's Mojave Desert—Muroc, an AAF airfield hard by the expanse of Rogers Dry Lake. Covering an area of 65 square miles, the smooth lake bed offered a comfortable margin for error to pilots landing unproved aircraft.

The X-1 arrived at Rogers Dry Lake in October of 1946. Jack Woolams had been killed earlier in the year while flying a special racing plane. Into his place stepped Chalmers ''Slick'' Goodlin, a 23-year-old former U.S. Navy pilot who had joined Bell after the War.

A shadow had been cast over the project by Woolams' death—and over the future of high-speed flight by the loss of one of Great Britain's finest test pilots, Geoffrey de Havilland. Son of the designer and aircraft manufacturer, he had been practicing to set a speed record in one of the company's experimental planes, the Swallow, when at nearly $9/10$ the speed of sound the jet began pitching wildly. Within seconds it had

disintegrated. Young de Havilland's death shocked the world aeronautical community. Perhaps the sound barrier was every bit as impenetrable as it seemed to be.

Bell and NACA intended for the X-1 to approach Mach 1 in steps of 15 to 20 miles per hour (a mere .02 or .03 Mach), hoping that the plane would warn them whether the next step would be fatal. And there were the 500 pounds of instruments aboard the X-1 to record everything that happened. "If we lost the airplane," said Walter Williams, who headed the NACA contingent at Muroc, "we could at least find out a little about what had happened."

The first powered flight of the X-1 was scheduled for December 6, 1946. Early that morning, the rocket plane was fastened to the B-29, fueled with alcohol and liquid oxygen and carried aloft, its orange sides frosting over as the supercold LOX inside the fuselage caused condensation to freeze on the outside. Descending to the X-1 and settling into the cockpit, Goodlin began his preflight check. Everything was going fine until he attempted to open the valve that pressurized the fuel tanks. Somehow, perhaps because of excess moisture, it had frozen shut.

Geoffrey de Havilland's three sons (from left, Peter, John and Geoffrey) examine the tail of a de Havilland Mosquito. Peter served as an executive of his father's company. John, the youngest son, and Geoffrey, the oldest, were both test pilots. John was killed in 1943 when the Mosquito he was flying collided with another; Geoffrey died in 1946 when his D.H.108 Swallow, second in a series of three, disintegrated in flight.

The third Swallow rakes the sky with its swept wings and tail fin during an early test. On September 6, 1948, this jet became the first British aircraft to exceed the speed of sound, reaching Mach 1.04.

Here was a mortal threat to the X-1. With the valve closed, the rocket engine could not function; nor could the propellants be jettisoned. Gliding the plane to a landing was out of the question. Full of fuel, it weighed more than its undercarriage could support. A crash would be inevitable.

Goodlin and the bomber's crew conferred anxiously and decided to land the B-29 with its explosive cargo attached. On the ground, Larry Bell watched with growing concern as the B-29 returned to Muroc. And then, for no apparent reason, the X-1's nosewheel swung out of its well, protruding below the B-29's undercarriage. If it locked in the down position, it would cause the bomber to crash, bringing both planes to a fiery end. The only alternative would be to jettison X-1. Goodlin, sitting in its cockpit, flipped the switch that operated the nosewheel as the B-29 approached the Muroc runway. Luckily, the wheel retracted just in time, and the B-29 gently touched down.

"Keep trying," Larry Bell said tersely to the X-1 team, before returning to Buffalo. And keep trying they did. Three days later, after care was taken to remove every trace of moisture from the fuel system, Goodlin completed the X-1's first powered flight. On the ground, an AAF observer noted that "a streak of flame came from the tail of the rocket" when the first unit was fired. Each combustion chamber was tested in turn and then Goodlin fired all four at once, shooting far ahead of a Lockheed P-80 jet fighter that had been sent up to photograph the event.

By early January, Goodlin had piloted the plane to a speed of Mach .8 at an altitude of 35,000 feet, reporting that the plane maintained "perfect control," with only "very slight shuddering" to indicate the onset of shock wave formation. By June of 1947, the Army Air Forces and NACA were ready to consider the next step.

Their decision would disappoint Slick Goodlin. It had been customary for the military services to let civilian test pilots fly new aircraft to their limits. But with the X-1 project demanding extensive government participation and Bell absolved of further responsibility for the airplane's performance, the AAF and NACA decided to take over. Goodlin was now out of the supersonic sweepstakes. He was replaced by a new and relatively unknown test pilot, Captain Charles E. "Chuck" Yeager, a 24-year-old World War II fighter ace from Hamlin, West Virginia.

Yeager represented the old school of test flying, for he was less an engineer than he was a superb pilot. Indeed, he had little formal technical training. But like the Wright brothers or Charles Lindbergh, he had a natural grasp of the dynamics of flight, and an ability to apply his understanding to flying. During the War, in his P-51 Mustang, Yeager had shot down 13 German warplanes, five in one day. After the War, he remained in the AAF, and in 1946 he became one of the first pilots to graduate from Flight Performance School, the Air Forces' test-pilot training school at Vandalia, Ohio. Yeager had proved an eager and apt pupil. In June 1947, when Colonel Albert Boyd, chief of flight testing for the AAF, had to choose Goodlin's replacement, he selected the stocky young captain. Yeager in turn picked two other fliers to work with him: test pilots Captain Jack Ridley, a fine engineer; and Lieutenant Bob Hoover, who would serve as backup pilot.

First, Yeager, Ridley and Hoover studied the X-1 at the Bell plant in Buffalo, where it had been brought for maintenance. There Bell engineer and test pilot Dick Frost ran a ground school for the military team. They became familiar with the rocket plane and its systems, and watched ground tests of its exotic rocket engine. In July, the three fliers and a crew headed by Major Robert Cardenas ferried the X-1, slung under the belly of the B-29 mother ship, back to Muroc.

During daytime meetings and informal evening discussions in the bar at Pancho's Fly Inn, a favorite night spot, Yeager and his fellow pilots speculated on the project and its chances for success. Yeager firmly believed that the X-1 could break the sound barrier. "I'd had a rifle as a boy," Yeager would recall decades later. "I knew that bullets went supersonic. And once in a while, I'd remember finding a bullet I'd fired lying underwater at the edge of a pond. You could see that it wasn't distorted or anything. So I didn't think anything funny would happen to me." But before Yeager could test this hypothesis, he would have to learn how to handle the X-1, and that meant flying it first as a glider.

Yeager's confidence in the aircraft showed itself immediately. On his first flight, he performed a slow roll during the glide to earth; on the next day, he did a two-turn spin. On his third and last flight, he playfully engaged chase pilot Bob Hoover in a mock dogfight almost all the

Civilian test pilot Chalmers "Slick" Goodlin leans jauntily against the X-1 he put through early tests at Muroc, California. Goodlin autographed the picture for Florence "Pancho" Barnes, the colorful owner and hostess of the Fly Inn, a favorite watering hole for Muroc fliers.

way down to landing. "Like nothing I've ever flown," said Yeager of the small rocket plane.

Late in August, Yeager prepared himself for his first powered flight. He christened the X-1 *Glamorous Glennis,* after his wife, just as he had his Mustang during the War. On August 29, the plane dropped away from the B-29 high over the Mojave Desert near Muroc. Yeager was supposed to hold the X-1 to no more than Mach .8, but the young pilot exuberantly rolled and dived the rocket plane, allowing it to reach Mach .85, the boundary where reliable aerodynamic data started to run out. Yeager expected a reprimand and he soon got it; Colonel Boyd, back at Wright Field, chastised him in writing, noting that neither plane nor pilot was expendable. "So please," urged Boyd, "approach higher speeds progressively and safely to the limit of your best judgment." And this Yeager did, on every flight thereafter.

There was an air of confidence at Muroc. As Richard Frost, Bell's flight-test director for the X-1 project, said: "If it could be done, we knew we could do it." But anticipation was tempered by the awareness that the X-1 was approaching a great void. Even enthusiasts like NACA's Walt Williams admitted to "a very lonely feeling as we began to run out of data."

On one flight, when the X-1 reached Mach .88, it experienced the rapid buffeting that other airplanes encountered at much lower air speeds. But the X-1 had been built so sturdily that there was no danger of its being shaken apart. A more disturbing question was whether Yeager would be able to control the pitch of his aircraft as it edged closer to the sound barrier.

Pilots from Muroc gather around the piano at Pancho Barnes's Fly Inn. A former barnstormer, Pancho—seen here with Air Force test pilot Chuck Yeager to her left—earned her nickname in the 1920s when she ran guns for Mexican revolutionaries.

On each test flight Yeager rolled *Glamorous Glennis* upside down and pulled the control column back to try out the plane's elevators. They had always worked satisfactorily, sending the aircraft diving toward the ground. But when Yeager attempted this maneuver one day at Mach .94, the results were unexpected and alarming: Nothing happened. The elevators had no effect whatsoever on the plane's attitude. Yeager wisely shut down the X-1's engine and glided back to a landing at Muroc.

NACA engineers studied the data from the flight and came to a disturbing conclusion. At Mach .94, a shock wave formed in front of the elevators, negating their effectiveness. It was time now to try the extra control authority that had been built into the plane.

On the 10th of October, 1947, *Glamorous Glennis* dropped away from the B-29 mother ship on its eighth powered flight. Yeager ignited the four chambers of the rocket engine, and the X-1 climbed away, trailing its usual thick stream of vapor. As arranged, Bob Hoover cruised along in a P-80 Shooting Star, 10 miles ahead of the launch point. Yeager quickly roared past him as the X-1 reached Mach .94. Yeager repeated the maneuver that had revealed the elevator problem on the earlier flight, only this time he flicked the stabilizer trim switch as well as pulling back on the control column. The plane plunged into a dive. "As far as I was concerned," recalled Yeager, "we had the thing licked."

So far the flight had proceeded without a hitch, but as Yeager started his gliding descent, the inside of the canopy began frosting over. The X-1's cockpit was always uncomfortably cold from the frigid liquid-oxygen tank just behind it. On this day water vapor, perhaps from an unusual amount of humidity in the air trapped inside the cockpit before the flight, condensed and froze. Try as he might, Yeager could not scrape away the frost. Hoover slid in close alongside the X-1 and began to radio instructions to Yeager, guiding him toward Muroc. With the chase pilot talking him down, Yeager made a gentle, blind landing on Rogers Dry Lake.

Yeager was in for a pleasant surprise the next day. Though his Machmeter had indicated Mach .94, it had not been working properly. Postflight analysis of data provided by radar tracking indicated that *Glamorous Glennis* had actually achieved a velocity of Mach .997, infinitesimally close to the speed of sound.

Before dawn on Tuesday, October 14, 1947, technicians set to work readying the X-1 for another flight. They recalibrated instruments and began to fuel the rocket plane with about 300 gallons each of alcohol and liquid oxygen.

Yeager was not in the best condition that October morning. Following his flight the preceding Friday, he and Glennis had ridden horseback through the desert night. On their return, Yeager failed to see a gate locked across the corral. His horse hit the gate, bolted, and threw the pilot off; Yeager landed heavily.

An officer braces for the blast that will shoot him up a 105-foot-tall steel tower at 40 mph. The seat and rig, built by Britain's Martin-Baker Aircraft Company, were tested with dummies first to ensure that the shock of ejection would not exceed human tolerance.

A "bang seat" for high-speed bailouts

On November 1, 1946, as a U.S. Navy bomber droned along 5,000 feet above Lakehurst, New Jersey, Lieutenant Al Furtek popped suddenly from the gunner's position, riding the latest airplane escape device—an ejection seat.

Emergency exit from aircraft had always been risky. G-forces could trap a pilot in a spinning plane. If he got out, he could smash into the tail. Swift jet aircraft under development in the 1940s would only increase the hazard.

The Navy adopted the new "bang seat," as pilots came to call the device that shot them clear of the plane. Early models could be used only above 1,000 feet and required the pilot to jettison the seat and pull his parachute's rip cord. Later seats performed these functions automatically and were so powerful that a pilot could eject even at ground level.

A simulated ejection shows how the seat appears before (top) and after partial extension (right). The seat would fire automatically when the pilot pulled down a canvas curtain to protect his face against the high-speed airstream.

Lieutenant Furtek punches out of a Douglas JD-1 bomber in the Navy's first live test of an ejection seat. A drogue parachute deployed when Furtek was 20 feet above the plane; half a second later, the seat's main chute billowed open. Furtek unbuckled himself, pushed away from the seat and floated down under his own parachute to an uneventful landing.

Air Force Major Chuck Yeager, the first man to fly faster than the speed of sound, emerges from a late version of the X-1. "People were real surprised that we had done it," he said after his historic flight, "and to find that my ears didn't fall off or anything."

The next day, in considerable pain and fearing that he might have broken a rib, Yeager drove to nearby Rosamond to consult a civilian doctor. He knew that if he went to the Air Force flight surgeon at Muroc, he would most likely be grounded. The doctor confirmed Yeager's fears—the pilot had two broken ribs on his right side. Yeager had the doctor tape them up and returned to Muroc, stoically enduring the pain.

Yeager's fall soon became common knowledge around Muroc, but no one realized how badly he had been hurt. And the pilot would have confided in no one, except that he faced a serious problem. He had to lock the hatch of the X-1 with his right hand, and he feared that he could not operate the latch because of the pain from his ribs. So on the morning of the flight, Yeager told Jack Ridley, his closest friend on the X-1 team, about his predicament. Realizing what the flight meant to Yeager, Ridley agreed to keep Yeager's secret. Ridley had a nine-inch length cut from a broom handle so that Yeager could reach the latch with his left hand. Thus equipped, Yeager boarded the B-29 mother ship.

At 10:02 a.m., with the bright sun already well into the sky, the B-29 roared to life. The bomber swept down the runway and lifted gracefully into the air. On the ground, Muroc's commanding officer, Colonel Signa Gilkey, closed the field to all other air traffic.

When the B-29 reached 5,000 feet, Yeager left the cavernous bomb bay for the tiny confines of *Glamorous Glennis*. Assisted by Jack Ridley, he squirmed and twisted his way into the cold cockpit, a stab of pain punctuating each movement. Ridley placed the hatch in its opening, and Yeager, assisted by the broom handle, locked it shut. Then he set about readying the X-1 for flight.

Five minutes before launch, Yeager pressurized the fuel tanks with nitrogen gas and checked the fuel-jettison system. Then he waited for the drop, hunched in the cold, his ribs throbbing. One minute before release, Jack Ridley asked, "You all set?" "Hell, yes," replied Yeager, "let's get it over with." At 10:26 a.m., 20,000 feet above the desert, Bob Cardenas intoned the now-familiar countdown and set *Glamorous Glennis* free into the bright blue sky.

Heavy with fuel, the X-1 plunged quickly earthward as Yeager's gloved hands flipped the switches that triggered half its rocket power. Under 3,000 pounds of thrust, the X-1 began to climb. Yeager kicked in the remaining two chambers, and with full power, the plane shot skyward. As the velocity increased, Yeager checked the effectiveness of the controls. They were functioning perfectly.

During the climb he had shut down two of the rocket's chambers while he checked over the aircraft. Now, at 42,000 feet and in approximately level flight, Yeager fired one of the two unlit chambers. Having consumed most of its fuel, the lightened X-1 accelerated rapidly. In the cockpit, the Machmeter wound steadily toward .98, touched it, then abruptly jumped off the scale. The instrument's spasm indicated that the nose of the X-1 had passed through its own shock wave. Yeager had just broken the sound barrier. On the ground, a new sound heralded Yeager's achievement. A sonic boom lashed the Mojave with a loud double crack. It was as startling and evocative of an era as the abrupt opening chords of Beethoven's *Eroica*.

The buffeting of the X-1 stopped; the plane became easier to control. Yeager shut down the engine, jettisoned the propellants remaining in the tanks, then began the glide to Muroc, the cold silence of the cockpit disturbed only by the sound of air flowing past the plane and the ticking of the cockpit clock.

Colonel Gilkey telegraphed news of success to Wright Field: CONFIDENTIAL PRIORITY. XS1 BROKE MACH NO ONE AT 42000 FT ALT. FLT CONDITIONS IMPROVED WITH INCREASE OF AIRSPEED. DATA BEING REDUCED AND WILL BE FORWARDED WHEN COMPLETED. END.

But the world would not hear of Yeager's accomplishment right away; the flight was of such military value that it would be kept secret for eight months. That night Yeager and a few cronies celebrated alone at Pancho's, where the owner treated them to a free steak.　～

Man-made tempests for aerodynamic research

Of all the tools employed by aeronautical engineers, the wind tunnel is by far the most important; without it aviation would still be languishing in the scientific Dark Ages.

The first wind tunnel was invented in 1871 by Francis Wenham, a marine engineer who was fascinated by the notion of powered flight. Wenham employed a steam-driven fan to force wind past a model wing mounted on a scale in a chamber 10 feet long and just 18 inches square. By reading the scale, he was able to measure precisely the lift generated by the wing. Contrary to popular speculation about flying, the lift proved much greater than the drag; powered flight seemed more possible than ever before.

More than three decades later, the Wright brothers employed a wind tunnel of their own devising to test 200 airfoils before building and launching their pioneering craft in 1903. Wind tunnels have been used ever since to explore aeronautical concepts and detect design flaws.

That models tested in wind tunnels yield accurate predictions of how planes will perform in flight is due largely to a formula worked out in 1883 by British physicist Osborne Reynolds. He combined several factors—including the distance between the leading and trailing edges of a plane's wing, the plane's speed and the density of the surrounding air—to arrive at a figure, known as the Reynolds number. For accurate wind-tunnel results, the test model's Reynolds number must equal that of the full-scale plane.

Small, slow-flying planes have small Reynolds numbers that are easy to match in the wind tunnel. But duplicating the huge Reynolds numbers of large, fast planes can pose staggering problems. Models of such aircraft must be of small scale to fit inside a wind tunnel; the smaller the scale, the more conditions inside the tunnel must compensate.

The most direct solution is to build behemoth wind tunnels, such as the yawning cave at left, so that larger models can be used. Yet this approach is extremely costly. To avoid such expense, aerodynamicists often use more modest wind tunnels and small-scale models of large planes, then raise the Reynolds number in the tunnel by pressurizing the air, as in the Variable Density Tunnel overleaf, or cooling it to increase the density of the wind. Alternatively, a denser gas—nitrogen or Freon—may be substituted for air. By combining these techniques, scientists can create wind-tunnel conditions that mimic actual flight conditions for a full-sized aircraft operating near, at or even well above the speed of sound.

Pinioned securely in the 30-by-60-foot test section of the largest wind tunnel at Langley Field, Virginia, a model of a supersonic jet is readied for a testing of low-speed flight characteristics. A pair of 4,000-hp fans behind the model suck air through the test section at 118 mph.

Wind tunnels from the Wrights to NASA

When the Wright brothers built their first wind tunnel in 1901, they made a mistake: They mounted the fan, which produced a wind of 35 mph, so that it would blow air into the apparatus, rather than suck air through it. This arrangement caused turbulence that affected the results of their experiments.

The Wrights and later wind-tunnel designers never made that error again. Moreover, most wind tunnels nowadays, instead of sitting open in a room, have fully enclosed return passages for the air to keep it flowing smoothly. Fans that are hundreds of times more powerful than the one the Wrights used are able to create winds of twice the speed of sound and even faster.

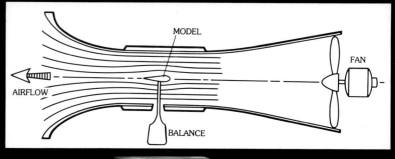

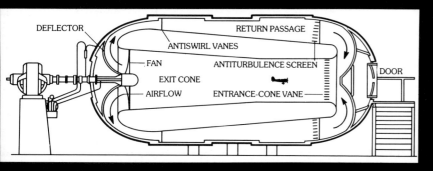

Mounted sturdily on cross-braced legs, the Wright brothers' wind tunnel, a replica of which is shown above and diagramed at top, made use of a two-bladed wooden fan to force air past a model wing inside the 16-by-16-inch test chamber.

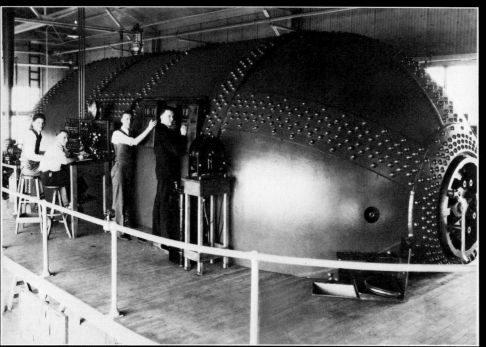

Massive rivets join the 2 ⅛-inch-thick steel plates of the Variable Density Tunnel, located at Langley. First used in 1923, the tunnel can be operated at 20 times atmospheric pressure to duplicate high Reynolds numbers. A pair of return ducts and a downstream fan (diagram, above) help to smooth out the airflow.

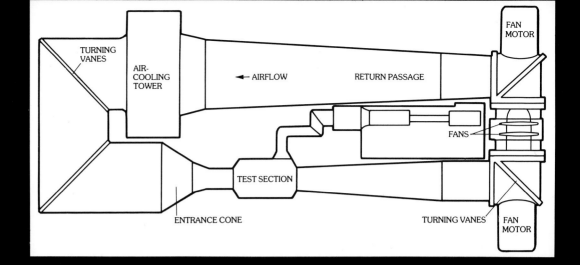

TURNING VANES

AIR-COOLING TOWER

TURNING VANES

FAN MOTOR

← AIRFLOW

RETURN PASSAGE

FANS

TEST SECTION

ENTRANCE CONE

TURNING VANES

FAN MOTOR

Langley's closed-loop facility (left) typifies modern wind-tunnel layout. On the inside (diagram, above) there are two 30,000-hp fans, a tapered return passage and a constricted entrance cone, all to ensure a smooth, powerful wind.

A massive set of turning vanes forms an ellipse 82 feet wide and 58 feet high at one corner of the Langley closed-loop wind tunnel. The vanes bend the airflow smoothly around the 90-degree turn and at the same time straighten out any vagrant eddies.

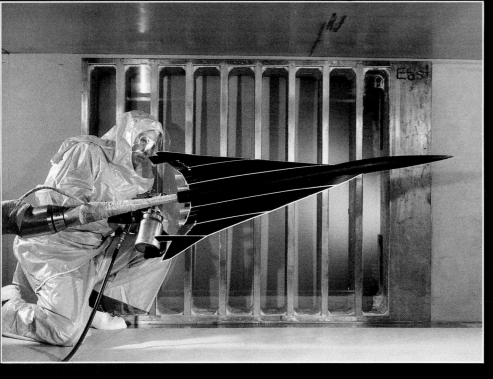

Clothed head to foot in protective garb, a technician applies a toxic solution to a model of an advanced supersonic transport. The chemical will evaporate wherever turbulence occurs in the Mach 4.6 winds of this tunnel.

Laser beams flash across a jet-engine intake cone at Langley. The beams are capable of measuring turbulence by detecting the motions of fine dust particles that are present in the airstream.

Solving puzzles of high-speed flight

As airplanes approached the speed of sound, designers needed answers to a range of questions that had never come up before. What happens as aircraft pass Mach 1—or fly much faster? How could the rapid oscillations called flutter, induced by high-speed flight, be moderated to make dives and other punishing combat maneuvers safer? How could the performance-robbing effects of shock waves be alleviated?

Wind-tunnel builders responded to these problems with ever more complex designs. Tunnels were built with vertical sections so that models could be tested in dives and tailspins. Ventilated tunnels were constructed to test engines operating under flight conditions. In some tunnels, tanks of compressed air were substituted for fans; when the air was released, it slammed through the tunnel much faster than any wind a fan could produce. And in some extremely advanced facilities, artillery pieces were used to blast models into a rushing airstream, effectively combining the velocities of the shot and the stream to study flight at speeds beyond Mach 5—if only for a fraction of a second per test.

The white panel on this airplane wing is a device designed to dampen flutter, an effect that is aggravated by the two missiles near the tip. The test is being conducted in a transonic wind tunnel at Langley.

An F-16 fighter model recovers from a tailspin as it falls through a 25-foot vertical tunnel. Such tests not only suggest design changes to reduce the likelihood of spins, but aid pilots in recovery techniques.

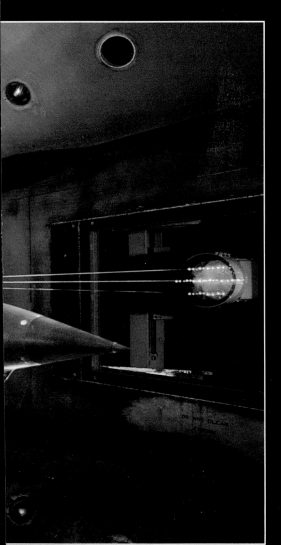

By capturing the refraction of light passing from denser to thinner air, a schlieren (German for striation) photograph reveals a shock wave at the nose of a model spacecraft.

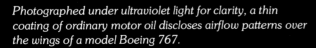

Photographed under ultraviolet light for clarity, a thin coating of ordinary motor oil discloses airflow patterns over the wings of a model Boeing 767.

Colored whirls behind a Boeing 737 wing reveal a trail of turbulence. The pattern is formed by a sensor that swings near the model and blinks in three colors, depending on air pressure.

Tracing invisible currents of air

Scientists employ ingenious methods to monitor invisible currents of air flowing around test shapes in wind tunnels. In the past smoke was regularly injected into the airstream to study the eddies swirling around models. While smoke is still used for some tests, more precise data can be obtained in less time with the three advanced methods shown here.

Each of these provides an indirect way to locate regions of varying air pressure and photograph the results. Later, if necessary, designers can order changes in the shape of a wing or fuselage to eliminate pockets of drag-inducing turbulence that show up in the photographs.

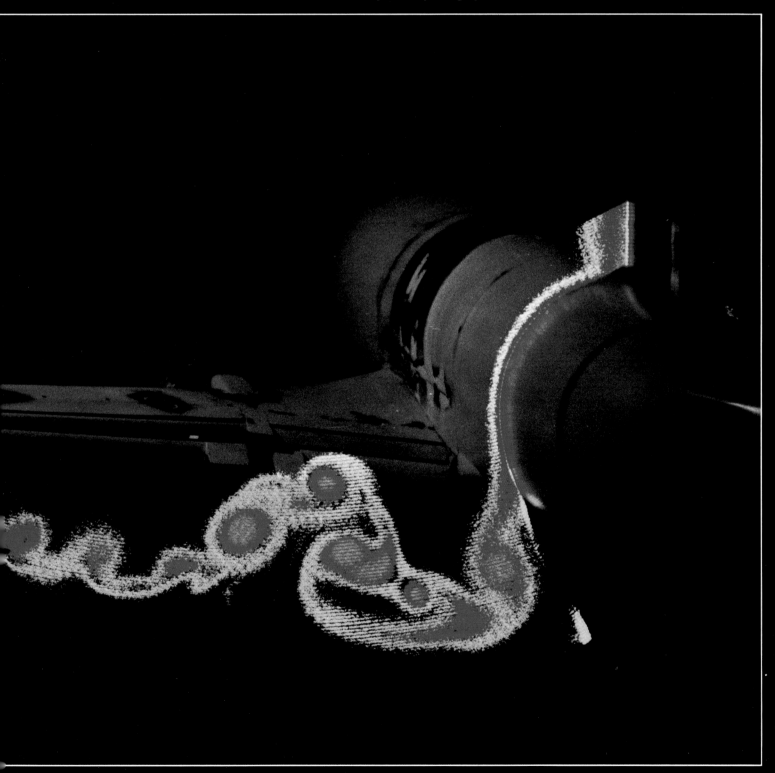

State of the art in aircraft design, Lockheed's YF-12A sits on the ramp at Edwards Air Force Base preparatory to flight in 1979.

5
"Different from anything the world has ever seen"

We have just won a war with a lot of heroes flying around in planes," said General Henry "Hap" Arnold, commander of the U.S. Army Air Forces. He had called his staff together in the Pentagon the morning after V-J Day to speak to them about the future of air warfare. Many in the audience had not yet recovered from the victory celebration of the previous night, but Arnold's speech would make them sit up and take notice.

"The next war may be fought by airplanes with no men in them at all," he continued. "It certainly will be fought with planes so far superior to those that we have now that there will be no basis for comparison. Take everything you've learned about aviation in the War, throw it out the window and let's get to work on tomorrow's aviation. It will be different from anything the world has ever seen."

Arnold's vision was based on solid fact. Even as he spoke, Bell designers were working on the X-1, the plane that heralded an era of creative experimentation and dazzling achievement. The X-1 was only the first in a series of so-called X-planes—flying laboratories equipped with powerful, fuel-gulping rockets that, for a few minutes at a time, would thrust them into supersonic flight. Test pilots returned from these brief excursions with data that designers readily applied to fast, new jets on their drawing boards.

By the late 1950s, the era of the supersonic X-planes would be all but over as production jet aircraft, benefiting from rocket-plane research, began flying at twice the speed of sound. By the mid-1960s, some superjets would routinely operate at Mach 3—more than 2,000 miles per hour—and at altitudes above 80,000 feet, performance that could hardly have seemed possible even to Hap Arnold, or to the men who first dreamed of supersonic flight before the War.

In October 1935, the world's leading aerodynamicists gathered in Rome, Italy, for a conference on high speeds in aviation. Italian dictator Benito Mussolini opened the meeting on a harsh note by announcing Italy's invasion of Ethiopia. Italian scientists, eager to show their progress in aerodynamics, conducted a tour of a laboratory where engineers were constructing a Mach 2.7 wind tunnel to study the effects of supersonic flight.

Against this backdrop, an obscure 34-year-old German engineer named Adolf Busemann presented a paper about a futuristic concept that would become the emblem of man's ability to fly faster than sound—the swept wing. As a child growing up in the port city of Lübeck, Busemann had been fascinated by the V-shaped wakes of ships. In his paper, he compared the shock wave created by an airplane in supersonic flight to the bow wave of a ship cutting through water. He took the analogy one step further: If the wings of a plane could be swept back, they would fall within the shock-wave cone streaming from the nose of the craft. Busemann theorized that this "arrow wing," as he called it, would thus have less drag than straight wings.

Busemann's paper attracted only a few polite comments at the conference. For one thing, swept wings were nothing new to aviation; before World War I, pioneer designers such as Britain's John Dunne had experimented with swept wings on tailless biplanes to enhance their stability. Furthermore, in the aeronautical climate of the mid-1930s—with jet engines not yet off the drawing boards and the propeller still king—supersonic flight seemed a long way off. British aerodynamicist W. F. Hilton calculated that a single-engined airplane would need 30,000 horsepower to fly faster than sound, a figure, he said, that "loomed like a barrier against future progress."

After Busemann had read his paper, Italy's General Arturo Crocco, organizer of the conference, sketched an aircraft on the back of a menu card. The plane had sweptback wings, a sweptback tail and a sweptback propeller to match. Crocco referred to it facetiously as "Busemann's airplane."

But in Germany, Busemann's theory would be regarded not as a joke but as a breakthrough. The Luftwaffe was experimenting eagerly with a number of provocative aircraft designs, and the engineer's work eventually caught the attention of Woldemar Voigt, senior designer at Messerschmitt. In 1942 Voigt decided to try out Busemann's idea in an experimental jet referred to as *Projekt 1101*. Its wings were to be angled back sharply—in marked contrast to the slightly swept wings on the Me 262 twin-engined jet fighter he was then developing. Work on *Projekt 1101* went forward in fits and starts, with Voigt unable to turn his full attention to it because of his involvement with the 262. Nevertheless, wind-tunnel tests on models of the sweptwing jet were so promising that in 1944 Voigt began development of a sweptwing research plane. But the war in Europe was over before it ever flew.

In the United States, scientist Robert T. Jones—unaware of Busemann's and Voigt's work—also began exploring swept wings for high-speed flight. The 35-year-old Jones, a college dropout, was a self-taught aerodynamicist who once had been a mechanic with a barnstorming troupe called the Marie Meyer Flying Circus. Later, while working in Washington, D.C., as an elevator operator at the Capitol, he had tutored a congressman eager to learn physics and higher mathematics. In 1934, the legislator, impressed with Jones's knowledge, got him a job at NACA as a junior engineer.

During the War, Jones was assigned to guided-weapons projects at

NACA's Langley laboratory. In January 1945, while working on the design for a flying bomb known as the Griswold Dart, Jones intuitively realized the advantage of a swept wing. At transonic and even supersonic speeds, the principles of physics that govern flight would dictate that, within the shock wave formed around a triangular wing, airflow would be subsonic.

Jones called his airflow theory "subsonic sweep," and following discussions with leading aerodynamicists, he received permission from NACA Director George Lewis to begin supersonic wind-tunnel tests. Several months of experimentation with different degrees of sweep confirmed Jones's airflow theories, and he recommended to his superiors at NACA that, in the future, swept wings be employed on all high-speed planes.

Before NACA could act on Jones's suggestion, Germany surrendered. Scientists and engineers were dispatched immediately to pick through its aeronautical research facilities. Among those who descended on Germany was Theodore von Kármán. While working at the California Institute of Technology, he had been consulted by Jones about sweptwing flight, and he had been skeptical. But now his doubts were about to vanish.

In mid-May 1945, von Kármán and a team of scientists arrived at a Luftwaffe laboratory near Brunswick where Adolf Busemann—working independently of Woldemar Voigt—had been doggedly pursuing his arrow-wing theory. In the laboratory, von Kármán and his men discovered models with swept wings, reams of wind-tunnel data—and Busemann himself.

"What is this business about sweepback?" von Kármán asked the German aerodynamicist.

"Oh, you remember," Busemann replied. "I read a paper on it at the Volta Congress in 1935."

Von Kármán and four other members of his team who had been at the congress did remember Busemann's paper, and they suddenly realized that Busemann and Robert Jones had been blazing the same trail. Von Kármán had little difficulty persuading Busemann to pursue his work in the United States, where he eventually joined the staff at NACA's Langley laboratory.

Scores of other German scientists and engineers, including Voigt, followed Busemann to the U.S., encouraged by a government recruiting drive called Operation *Paperclip*. Many of them eventually made telling contributions to American aviation, but it was Busemann's work that had the most immediate effect. Boeing, for example, scrapped plans for a straight-wing jet bomber to build one with swept wings. The resulting plane, the XB-47, was the forerunner of a whole class of jet bombers and commercial transports. Similarly, designers at North American Aviation, then developing a straight-wing fighter known as the XP-86 for the Army Air Forces, changed course and angled back its wings, producing the graceful and nimble aircraft that was to be-

A Boeing B-47, the world's first sweptwing jet bomber, climbs after takeoff in 1956. The Stratojet's 35-degree wing sweep helped give it a top speed of more than 600 mph, so fast that admiring pilots called it "a six-engine fighter."

come famous as the Sabre. Sweeping back the Sabre's wings, commented aviation historian Ray Wagner, changed it "from a mediocre fighter into a great one."

On October 1, 1947—two weeks before Chuck Yeager cracked the sound barrier in the Bell X-1—the sweptwing version of the XP-86 was ready for its first flight at Muroc. The man who was to pilot the jet was George Welch, who had won fame during World War II as the first American pilot to engage the enemy at Pearl Harbor. He went on to score 16 kills in the Pacific before joining North American as a test pilot in 1944.

On the morning of October 1, Welch made a few taxiing runs in the XP-86, then took off into the clear California sky for what was supposed to be a 10-minute familiarization flight. But when Welch came in to land, he could not get the plane's nose wheel all the way down. For the next 40 minutes, he joggled and maneuvered the craft in an effort to jar the wheel into position, but to no avail. Finally, he decided to ease the plane down in a nose-high landing. When the main wheels hit the ground, the impact jolted the nose wheel down, and Welch brought the XP-86 to a safe stop.

The jammed nose wheel proved to be one of the rare snags in the XP-86 test program. Pilots who flew the Sabre prototype termed it a "dream airplane." And on April 26, 1948, less than a year after Yeager's historic flight in the X-1, Welch put the XP-86 into a shallow dive. The plane slipped past Mach 1, making it the first aircraft designed for combat to break the sound barrier.

The Soviets had also been working on a sweptwing jet. Using captured German data as the Americans did, designers Artem Mikoyan and Mikhail Gurevich produced a trim little fighter they designated

Four North American F-100 Super Sabres of the U.S. Air Force Thunderbirds aerobatics team streak overhead in diamond formation during a 1953 training mission. With a top speed of 864 mph, the Super Sabre was the first operational U.S. jet that was capable of reaching supersonic speeds in level flight.

the MiG-15. On December 30, 1947, three months after the XP-86's first flight, a Soviet test pilot took off in the MiG. Soon, designers in other countries followed suit: France's Marcel Dassault developed the Mystère in 1951, while Britain's Sidney Camm produced the Hawker Hunter in 1953. Yet none of these early sweptwing jets could reach Mach 1 in level flight. This was the next great challenge facing designers and engineers. Surmounting it would require more powerful engines and even sleeker airframes.

Less than a year after George Welch took up the XP-86 for the first time, designers at North American had begun work on a plane they hoped would be able to fly and fight at supersonic speeds. They named it the Sabre 45 because its wings were angled back at 45 degrees. It took the North American design team, headed by engineer Ray Rice, five years to move the Sabre 45 from drawing board to runway. By the time the jet was ready to fly in the summer of 1953, the Sabre 45 had acquired a new designation, the YF-100.

For a power plant, the plane had a Pratt & Whitney J57 turbojet. This new engine produced nearly five tons of thrust and boasted a novel feature, an afterburner in the tailpipe. This device burned fuel squirted into the exhaust to deliver another 5,000 pounds of thrust for takeoff and combat.

The wings of the YF-100 spanned only 37 feet. They were swept back more sharply by 10 degrees than the wings of the F-86, and they were more than 50 per cent thinner to reduce drag even further. The plane's tail fin also was thin and sharply raked back. And the YF-100's fuselage was equally streamlined—a long, slender body with a bubble canopy that barely broke the plane's smooth lines.

On the morning of May 25, 1953, the YF-100 was ready for its first flight. George Welch, now North American's chief test pilot, strode confidently out to the plane at Edwards Air Force Base, formerly Muroc. The base had been renamed to honor test pilot Glen Edwards, killed in the 1948 crash of a Northrop YB-49 flying-wing bomber.

Welch clambered up a ladder into the YF-100's cockpit and strapped himself in. He had been instructed, if all was going well with the flight, to try to push the plane past the speed of sound. As Welch prepared to take off, he called out to Lieutenant Colonel Frank "Pete" Everest, the Air Force test pilot who would be flying chase in an F-86. If the YF-100 exceeded Mach 1 that morning, Welch promised, he would buy the beer afterward.

Welch raced the jet across the hard-baked clay of Rogers Dry Lake and into the air, with Everest close behind. The new fighter and the F-86 rose swiftly into the sky, the experimental plane easily out-climbing the older jet. "Turn her loose," Everest radioed Welch. Moments later, at 35,000 feet, Welch said, "Hang on, here we go." He pushed the YF-100's throttle into the afterburner position and shot away from the Sabre, trailing a streamer of bright golden flame. A few seconds later, Welch radioed "Bingo"—the YF-100 had become the world's first jet intended for production to exceed the speed of sound in level flight.

A week later, Pete Everest set a low-altitude speed record in the YF-100, flying 755 miles per hour at just over 100 feet. But he was not happy with the plane, noting that he had found "unstable tendencies at high and low speeds." The problem occurred in maneuvering. High-speed turns caused the jet to skid sideways. At low speeds, a bank in one direction brought on a phenomenon called adverse yaw—the plane tended to turn right when the pilot wanted to go left, and vice versa. Either trait, if it caught a pilot off guard, could cause a crash. Yet Everest's complaint went unheeded; as he later recalled, "North American took exception to my negative report and assured Air Force headquarters that the airplane was safe to fly." Over Everest's objections, the Air Force pronounced the plane, by now known as the Super Sabre, ready for production. By September 1954, several squadrons—70 planes—were in service with no hint of trouble.

Meanwhile, the X-series of rocket planes continued to carry pilots higher and faster than ever before. The Bell X-2, a sweptwing advance on the X-1 with a 15,000-pound-thrust engine, was commissioned in 1946. Its goal was to reach Mach 3, a task demanding so much preliminary research that the X-2 would not fly until 1955. Before then, the Douglas X-3 was well under way. A gleaming white aircraft known as the Flying Stiletto for its long, pointed fuselage, the X-3 was jet powered, and its purpose was more modest: to prove that a jet could sustain a speed of Mach 2. With stubby wings spanning just 23 feet, it first flew on October 15, 1952.

Test pilots complained that the X-3 had a handling problem similar to the one that Pete Everest reported in the F-100. On one occasion, when

French designer Marcel Dassault, the creator of a long line of distinguished military aircraft, stands beside his Ouragan jet fighter prototype in 1949. His company, which was founded in 1946, became one of the leading developers and producers of aircraft in the Western world.

Nearly two decades of development are represented in this photograph of Dassault jets, taken at a company airfield in 1967. From the top, they are the Ouragan (1949), Mystère IV (1952), Super-Mystère B2 (1955), Etendard IV (1956), Mirage III (1956) and Mirage V (1967)—all fighters— and the Mirage IV bomber (1959).

NACA test pilot Joe Walker put the X-3 into a roll near Mach 1, the plane corkscrewed out of control, twisting and tumbling about all three axes. The violent stresses threatened to break the X-3 apart, but Walker managed to regain control of the craft and land it. Such behavior was unacceptable in any airplane. Eventually the X-3, which never reached Mach 2, was retired to become, in the words of one pilot, "a glamorous hangar queen, useful mainly for publicity photographs."

Not long after Walker's close call, the F-100 showed that—as Everest had warned—it too could turn on its pilot. On October 12, 1954, George Welch, who had praised the Super Sabre as "one of the easiest and nicest" planes he had ever flown, was diving an F-100 to test its handling characteristics at Mach 1.5 when the plane abruptly side-slipped and slued out of control. The crew of a B-47 flying in the area saw the F-100 turn over and plummet earthward. At 2,000 feet, it disintegrated; George Welch had no chance to bail out.

Search teams scoured the desert to retrieve fragments of the plane for analysis. Then, armed with the data from Welch's crash and from Walker's near-fatal flight in the X-3, North American and NACA scientists began studying the control problems that seemed inherent in both planes. By now so many F-100s were in service or on order that whatever the problem was, it had to be found and fixed. The investigators soon realized that to prevent violent, uncontrollable movements during rolls and turns beyond Mach 1, planes needed taller tail fins, increased wing span and sensitive damping devices. As a consequence, the wing span of the Super Sabre was increased from 37 feet to 39 feet, the tail fin was made 13 inches higher, and equipment was installed that stopped an incipient skid quicker than most pilots could react to it. As for the adverse yaw, pilots simply had to be careful when turning at low speed. With these remedies, the F-100 proved to be a dependable aircraft.

A year and a half after the fighter went into service, an accident involving one Super Sabre provided information on a subject that obviously could not be tested—the ability of a man to survive ejection at supersonic speeds. On February 26, 1955, test pilot George Smith took an F-100 up for a routine post-production test flight. As Smith was cruising over the Pacific Ocean off Palos Verdes, his F-100 suddenly nosed down and went into an uncontrollable dive. Smith tried to pull back on the stick, but he could not budge it. As the jet plunged earthward, a chase-plane pilot radioed frantically, "George, bail out."

Barely five seconds from impact—at an altitude of 6,000 feet and a speed of Mach 1.05—Smith jettisoned his canopy and ejected. The supersonic slip stream slammed him with 64 Gs for a fraction of a second, ripping off his helmet and oxygen mask and knocking him unconscious. Smith's parachute opened automatically, and he landed in the ocean, where a fishing boat rescued him.

Five days later, the pilot awoke in the hospital with severe internal injuries. His last memory, he told investigators, was of the needle on his

Designer Ed Heinemann (left), father of Douglas Aircraft's Mach 2 D-558-2 Skyrocket, checks blueprints in the California firm's famed El Segundo design bullpen. In just a few years after World War II, said Heinemann, aircraft designers moved "from nonglamorous transports and prop-driven attack planes to the sleek and swift machines which licked at the frontiers of space."

Machmeter pointing at 1.05. Later, it was determined that the plane's hydraulic control systems had failed.

Smith recovered, and six months after his mishap he returned to work testing F-100s. The accident proved that ejection at supersonic speeds, though not necessarily fatal, imposed tremendous stresses on a pilot. Soon engineers were hard at work designing flight suits, crash helmets and oxygen masks that would better resist wind blast.

With the F-100, Mach 1 had become commonplace, and designers turned to the next challenge for a production aircraft—Mach 2. The Douglas Skyrocket, another rocket-propelled research aircraft, had proved in 1953 that such a speed was possible. But for a practical aircraft to sustain Mach 2 with the power available from the jet engines of the mid-1950s, drag would have to be dramatically reduced.

The answer to that problem lay with Richard Travis Whitcomb, a

The seven most important experimental designs of the early 1950s stand on the checkered tarmac of Edwards Air Force Base. In the center is the dartlike Douglas X-3. Surrounding it, clockwise from lower left, are the Bell X-1A, the Douglas D-558-1, the Convair XF-92A, the Bell X-5, the Douglas D-558-2 and the Northrop X-4.

Shaped like a flying saucer, Avro's Avrocar carried a two-man crew under twin bubble canopies. An advanced version was to have had a top speed of 300 mph and a range of about 1,000 miles.

Conceived as a shipborne fighter, the XFY-1 had a delta wing and a ventral fin that could be jettisoned for emergency landings. The pilot entered the cockpit by means of a 20-foot ladder wheeled alongside.

The first of the only two Bell X-22s ever built crashed five months after its inaugural flight, but by 1983 the one below had flown nearly 500 times.

Valiant attempts at vertical flight

After the War, a small number of aircraft designers in Europe and the United States tackled the problem of creating machines with the capacity for vertical takeoffs and landings (VTOL). These were not to be helicopters, but fixed-wing aircraft with the speed of planes that operated from runways.

Such craft were not feasible before the invention of the gas turbine engine; piston engines weighed too much for the power they produced. But even with plenty of power available, how best to use it was far from obvious.

The most straightforward approach was taken by the designers of the Convair XFY-1 Pogo *(far left)*. A turboprop engine turned two propellers that rotated in opposite directions. This prevented the engine from spinning the plane slowly like a top. The Pogo worked, but not very well. Said one pilot of backing down to land on the four casters that supported the craft, "It's awful hard to fly an airplane looking over your shoulder."

The saucer-shaped Canadian Avrocar was less successful. Powered by three turbojets driving a large ducted fan at its core, it rose on a cushion of air then scooted along a few feet above the ground. Its designers hoped that future models could fly at higher altitudes on the lift generated by the airfoil shape of the fuselage, but the Avrocar reportedly was so difficult to control that the project was scrapped.

The most successful concept embodied the principle of vectored thrust by which jet-driven fans could be directed vertically for takeoff, then rotated 90 degrees for horizontal flight. Starting in the late 1950s, experiments with such a system have led to an operational fighter—the British Aerospace Harrier—and to the Bell X-22A, a highly sophisticated research craft used to explore the far reaches of vertical flight.

junior engineer at NACA. Whitcomb had joined the agency in 1943 after reading an article about it in *Fortune*. Over the following years, he worked on a variety of projects involving high-speed flight. Then in 1951, he and several other NACA scientists were assigned to probe the mysteries of drag at speeds approaching Mach 1 and beyond in Langley's new transonic wind tunnels, which had entered service in the late 1940s. While testing various models, they found themselves confronted with an odd phenomenon: The actual drag of models at transonic speeds was much greater than the predicted drag.

Whitcomb was stymied by these findings. He began poring over photographs of shock waves forming on wind-tunnel models. The photographs, made with a special set of lights and lenses, "were giving me fits," he recalled. "None of them looked as they should." Besides forming at the noses of the models, shock waves also appeared behind the wings. These extra shock waves accounted for the unexpected drag. But what to do about them?

The best shape for a high-speed aircraft was generally considered to be that of a so-called ideal streamlined body, a bullet-like shape that produced less drag than any other. No airplane attained that ideal—compromises invariably had to be made for wings, tail and canopy—but designers tried to come as close as they could. They gave the fuselage a pointed nose, then gradually thickened the body—that is, increased the cross-sectional area—until the fuselage reached its maximum diameter near the middle. The tail end of the fuselage then began to decrease in diameter.

It struck Whitcomb one day that this approach was wrong. After further thought, he arrived at what he called "a rule of thumb, a sort of basic principle: Transonic drag is a function of the longitudinal development of the cross-sectional areas of the entire plane." Put another way, it was not the diameter of the fuselage alone that mattered. It was the cross-sectional area of the fuselage combined with that of the wings or tail at a given point that should equal the corresponding cross-sectional area of the ideal streamlined shape. Wings, for example, add to the aircraft's cross-sectional area; to compensate, the fuselage should be made narrower where the wings join it.

Whitcomb was certain that he had accounted for the puzzling data emanating from Langley's wind tunnels. But now he had to put his theory, which he called the area rule, before Langley's select technical seminar. If it could stand up to the scrutiny of NACA's senior staff, it would have passed its first hurdle. At the seminar's next meeting, Whitcomb spoke for 20 minutes. At the end of his presentation there was silence. Finally, Adolf Busemann stood up. Turning to his colleagues, the pioneer of sweptwing technology remarked, "Some people come up with half-baked ideas and call them theories. Whitcomb comes up with a brilliant idea and calls it a rule of thumb." There could have been no greater praise for Whitcomb's concept.

"Now I had to go prove it," said Whitcomb. After a series of experiments, he produced a model with a pinched-in fuselage that accomplished precisely what he had predicted it would. It virtually eliminated the troublesome rise in drag at transonic speeds. The next step was to see if the area rule would work for a real airplane.

The perfect candidate was the Convair YF-102. Designed as a Mach 1.5 interceptor, the stubby, delta-winged jet had thus far proved a disappointment. On its maiden flight in 1953, test pilot Dick Johnson was able to exceed Mach 1 only in a steep dive. Transonic drag had exceeded the 14,500 pounds of thrust available from the YF-102's Pratt & Whitney J57 engine.

Following Whitcomb's recommendations, Convair engineers redesigned the plane to make it more streamlined, lengthening the fuselage seven feet and pinching it along the wing roots. On December 21, 1954, Johnson took the redesigned jet up on a test flight; in the words of fellow pilot Pete Everest, the plane "slipped easily past the sound barrier and kept right on going." With its new-found speed, the YF-102A entered service as the F-102A Delta Dagger and would be flown for many years by the U.S. Air Force. In 1955, Whitcomb won aviation's highest award, the Collier Trophy, for his breakthrough.

With the validity of the area rule established, aircraft designers everywhere began applying it to the next generation of supersonic planes. Convair came up with the F-106 Delta Dart, which had a much more powerful engine than the Dagger. Lockheed produced the F-104 Starfighter. Powered by a General Electric J79 engine developing 15,800 pounds of thrust, the Starfighter was distinguished by short, razor-like wings with a thickness-to-chord ratio of just 3.36 per cent and swept leading edges. A pencil-thin fuselage made the jet look "as if it was going Mach 2 just sitting in the hangar," remarked one admiring pilot. On April 27, 1956, the Starfighter lived up to its promise, becoming the first jet to exceed Mach 2 in level flight. Not long afterward, it broke the sound barrier while climbing—the first jet of any kind to do so.

In September, the Air Force was ready to dare the next peak in the quest for greater speed—Mach 3. After 10 years of preliminaries, the Bell X-2 was at last ready to make that assault—and to attempt to reach the as yet unattained altitude of 100,000 feet.

To withstand the 750° F. heat predicted at three times the speed of sound, the X-2 was made of stainless steel and a copper-nickel alloy instead of the aluminum used for slower planes. Its rocket engine generated 800 pounds less thrust than the J79 engine in the F-104; consequently, the X-2 would be able to reach Mach 3 only in a dive. It was not a docile aircraft. The X-2 was so skittery, noted one observer, that there was "a calculated risk of losing the pilot and the aircraft" every time it was flown.

On July 23, 1956, Pete Everest, who had made several low-speed runs in the plane, flew the X-2 to a world's speed record of Mach 2.87. Seven weeks later, test pilot Captain Iven Kincheloe, a jet ace in Korea

A Convair F-102A shows the Coke-bottle contour of its fuselage; the constriction eliminated drag that had kept an earlier model from going supersonic. At right, NACA's Richard Whitcomb, who recommended reshaping the fuselage, points out the improvement to Air Force Secretary Donald Quarles.

and an accomplished engineer, set an altitude record in the rocket plane. Kincheloe flashed past the 100,000-foot mark as if he had done the same thing a dozen times before, ignoring a slight roll. Had he tried to correct it, he might easily have sent the plane out of control. The rocket engine exhausted its fuel, but the X-2, slowly rolling onto its side, continued to coast up to 126,200 feet, more than 35,000 feet higher than any man had flown before. Kincheloe reached Mach 2.6 on his earthward dive before the thicker atmosphere restored the effectiveness of his controls and allowed him to right the X-2 and glide safely to earth. The record-setting flight earned Kincheloe the title "First of the Spacemen" in the press. It was an apt description, for at the peak of his trajectory 90 per cent of the earth's atmosphere lay below him. He could make out the subtle arc of the earth's curvature; the sun was a bright spot in a blue-black sky.

The goal of achieving Mach 3 still remained. For this feat the Air Force selected test pilot Captain Milburn "Mel" Apt. Assigned to the X-2 program several months earlier, Apt had not yet flown the X-2 or any other rocket plane. Nonetheless, he was a veteran of supersonic flight in the F-100 and his skill and courage were unquestioned. Once, while flying a chase plane for a fellow test pilot, Apt followed a crippled jet toward the ground; when it crash-landed in the desert, Apt landed alongside and pulled its injured occupant from the burning wreckage, saving his life. Besides, Kincheloe was already busy planning the next high-speed research plane, the X-15 *(pages 146-147);* he would be available only to fly chase. Everest had been sent to the Armed Forces Staff College in Norfolk, Virginia. Apt was the man for the job.

On September 27, 1956, after several sessions in an X-2 flight simu-

X-15, herald of the space age

When the U.S.S.R. launched *Sputnik I* in 1957, America's hopes for a future in space rode heavily on a rocket-powered airplane called the X-15. Designed as the fastest X-plane, it was intended to fly at more than six times the speed of sound and reach altitudes above 200,000 feet.

When the Air Force, Navy and NACA had asked for such a craft in 1954, its specifications seemed unrealistically ambitious. "About all this airplane will do," predicted one designer to NACA officials, "is prove the bravery of the pilot." But others, notably North American Aviation's Chief Engineer Harrison Storms, were enthusiastic. His designers went to work, and in 1955 North American was chosen to build three of the planes.

On September 17, 1959, the X-15 was ready for its first powered flight. The event, recorded in the photographs on these pages, took place at Edwards Air Force Base in California. At the controls was test pilot Scott Crossfield. "As soon as I went supersonic," he recalled later, "it was obvious that this airplane was designed to fly at high speeds."

The X-15s went on to a nine-year career, setting record after record for winged aircraft. In 1963 test pilot Joe Walker flew one of the planes to an altitude of 354,200 feet, half again as high as originally planned. Four years later an X-15 set a speed record of 4,520 miles per hour—Mach 6.72. Both records still stood in 1983.

The X-15s were retired in 1968. By then they had aided in a vast range of endeavors, from photographing stars to testing equipment for the Apollo space program. But perhaps the X-15 will be best remembered for proving that a pilot could ascend above the earth's atmosphere and return safely to terra firma.

Attired in a pressure suit, test pilot Scott Crossfield prepares to enter the cockpit of the X-15, shackled snugly under the broad wing of a B-52 Stratofortress. As the bomber took off to launch the X-15 on its first powered flight, Crossfield was supremely confident. "I have first-class fare," he quipped over the radio, "and a private compartment."

Set loose from the B-52 at 38,000 feet, Crossfield fires the X-15's eight rocket chambers. Three minutes later, after reaching 50,000 feet and Mach 2.3, the X-15 had spent its 18,000 pounds of fuel, and Crossfield glided earthward to a landing.

The test flight over, Crossfield meets reporters. The seasoned pilot, responding humbly to the congratulations that greeted him, deferred to North American's chief engineer. "The success of a flight like this rests with the airplane," he said. "This is Harrison Storms' day."

lator, Apt was ready. As the mother ship, a B-50, carried the X-2 aloft, Apt mentally reviewed his instructions: He was to climb to 70,000 feet, then dive earthward in an attempt to reach Mach 3. If he encountered any stability problems, he was to decelerate at once. Above all, he was not to make any sudden control adjustments past Mach 2.7. If he did, the plane was likely to go out of control and then, as technicians had warned, "anything could happen."

At 25,000 feet, the B-50 released the X-2 and Apt switched on the plane's rocket engine. Flames shot from the exhaust and the X-2 accelerated rapidly, its pilot pressed against his seat by the sudden G-force.

"Start the nose up," radioed Iven Kincheloe, who was flying an F-86 chase plane. "You've got her, attaboy," he coached. "Looking real good. Okay, he's starting to climb now."

Kincheloe applied full throttle, but the X-2 sped easily away from him as Apt began his climb. At 70,000 feet, Apt nosed the X-2 over and began his dive. Seconds later, the X-2 reached Mach 3.2—2,094 miles an hour. So far, the flight was textbook smooth. After 140 seconds, the engine stopped, its fuel exhausted, and Apt radioed, "Okay, she's cut out. I'm turning."

But he was going too fast, and as he began to bank toward Edwards Air Force Base, the X-2 tumbled out of control. Apt yelled "She goes! . . ." and then was rendered unconscious by the plane's wild careening. When he came to, he realized he could not regain control and attempted to abandon the aircraft. He punched the ejection button and the entire nose, which was designed as an escape capsule, blew off. But as a small drogue parachute filled to slow the capsule and stabilize its fall, the shock of the sudden deceleration knocked Apt unconscious again. Before he could recover and bail out of the capsule using his own parachute, the nose of the X-2 slammed into the Mojave Desert, killing the pilot at once. Investigators pored over data from the flight, but never were able to determine why the pilot began the turn at such a high speed, sending the X-2 out of control. Mel Apt's death ended the X-2 program but not the lure of Mach 3 flight. The first practical plane to achieve it would prove a radical departure from the X-2. It would be powered by turbojets instead of rockets, and it would be able to fly at Mach 3 not for just minutes, but for hours at a time.

The man who successfully designed the revolutionary aircraft that such a lofty goal demanded was Lockheed's Clarence "Kelly" Johnson. Since designing the twin tail for the company's Electra in 1933, Johnson had become chief of Lockheed's Advanced Projects Development Group—a small, elite team of engineers that called itself the "Skunk Works," after a moonshine factory in the popular Li'l Abner comic strip. Under Johnson, the Skunk Works became famous for its innovative designs: the P-80 Shooting Star, the first American jet to see full-scale production; the Constellation, a triple-tailed, four-engined airliner that arguably was the most beautiful prop-driven transport ever

Clarence "Kelly" Johnson, Lockheed's legendary designer, admires a model of his Shooting Star, the first U.S. operational jet fighter. "I knew what I wanted to do when I was 12," he once said. "There has never been any change in my desire since that time to design airplanes."

Two of Johnson's most famous designs, the U-2 spy plane and the F-104 Starfighter, are seen above and at right. Early U-2s flew over the Soviet Union with virtual impunity until 1960. The F-104, for which Johnson won the Collier Trophy in 1954, was the first Mach 2 jet fighter.

built; and the so-called "missile with a man," the F-104 Starfighter.

In the summer of 1954, Lockheed suggested to the Air Force that it develop a spy plane, a photoreconnaissance aircraft that could cruise at very high altitudes and have the endurance to cross large portions of, say, the Soviet Union. The Air Force approved the idea, and Johnson and his engineers came up with an elegant design: the U-2. It had an 80-foot wing span to support it in the thin atmosphere above 60,000 feet and could carry so much fuel that it had a range of 4,000 miles.

In 1956, the U-2 began flying over the Soviet Union, far above Russian air defenses. But Johnson realized that Soviet advances in radar and surface-to-air missile technology eventually would make the "U-bird" vulnerable. He and his team studied ways to increase the survivability of the U-2, but soon concluded that the best course lay in developing a completely new reconnaissance airplane to keep ahead of Soviet technology. The plane Johnson envisioned would be able to cruise at Mach 3 above 80,000 feet.

In the spring of 1958, Johnson took a formal proposal for the new spy plane to the Air Force—and to the Central Intelligence Agency, which had become interested in the project. At the same time, the Navy and Convair proposed spy planes of their own, to be powered by ramjets—engines that have no compressor and rely on the speed of an aircraft to ram air into the combustion chamber. The Navy suggested developing such an aircraft and launching it from a balloon; because a ramjet will not operate at speeds of less than about 500 miles per hour, booster rockets would get the plane started. The idea proved unfeasible because the balloon would have had to measure a mile in diameter to lift the plane. Convair's proposal was barely more practical—a Mach 4 plane that would be carried aloft by a Con-

Seven who made the ultimate sacrifice

In 1937, Edmund T. "Eddie" Allen, the acknowledged dean of American test pilots, wrote that a good test pilot was a man "bent on reducing his risks, and capable of planning for every emergency that might occur." He could have been describing any of the men pictured here. Yet, despite the methodical caution with which these pilots approached their work, all of them died at the controls of the planes they flew for a living.

Some fell victim to experimental aircraft like the Bell X-2 or the Northrop flying wings, in spite of the best efforts of designers to make them safe. Others were betrayed by less exotic aircraft, either through obscure malfunctions that could not be foreseen, or in freak accidents during routine missions. But these men bequeathed to aviation a rich legacy of achievement: Through their courage, skill and professional élan, they set a standard for excellence that would inspire all who came after.

Eddie Allen piloted at least 80 different airplanes on their maiden flights during his career. He died when a B-29 prototype caught fire and crashed in 1943.

Lockheed's Milo Burcham, who made a name for himself testing the P-38 Lightning, was killed in the 1944 crash of a P-80 jet fighter.

Recognizing the danger of the task, Northrop paid Harry Crosby $15,000 in 1944 to test its MX-334 rocket-powered flying wing. He died in the crash of its successor, the XP-79, on its maiden flight.

Glen Edwards had a degree in aeronautical engineering before joining the Northrop YB-49 flying-wing program in 1948. He perished when a prototype of the bomber broke up in flight over the Mojave Desert.

Captain Milburn "Mel" Apt became the first pilot to exceed Mach 3 when his X-2 research craft hit 2,094 mph in 1956. In seconds, the plane lurched out of control and tumbled to earth.

X-2 pilot Captain Iven Kincheloe had been selected to fly the North American X-15 when he was killed in 1958 during a routine flight in an F-104.

In 1963 Joe Walker flew the X-15 to a record altitude of 354,200 feet. Three years later he died when his F-104 collided with an XB-70 bomber (pages 157-159).

vair B-58 supersonic bomber. The government rejected that plan because launching the craft from the B-58 at high speed seemed too complex and hazardous.

With Convair and General Dynamics out of the running, the government accepted Lockheed's proposal in January 1960, ordering the firm to construct in secret 12 prototypes of the design that the Skunk Works had named the A-12. The engines were to be high-performance turbo-jets equipped with afterburners that operated continuously to maintain Mach 3 flight. To sustain the engines, the plane would carry 80,000 pounds of fuel—more than 12,000 gallons. The plane would have a long and slender fuselage and stubby delta wings with leading edges that blended smoothly into chines—horizontal surfaces attached to the fuselage to increase lift.

During the two years it took to move the radical-looking A-12 from

U.S. Air Force test pilots Colonel Robert Stephens (front) and Colonel Daniel Andre perch on their Lockheed YF-12A on May 1, 1965. They had just set a speed record of 2,070.1 mph and an altitude record for sustained flight of 80,257.9 feet in the jet, an experimental fighter version of the SR-71 reconnaissance plane.

blueprints to prototype, Johnson recalled, "everything on the aircraft, from rivets and fluids up through materials and power plants, had to be invented from scratch." And the inventing had to be done quickly. For on May 1, 1960, the Soviets downed a U-2 piloted by Francis Gary Powers. Now it was more important than ever to build a reconnaissance plane that could fly so fast and so high as to be practically invulnerable. The Skunk Works redoubled its efforts.

The first problem that Johnson's designers encountered was what to build the A-12 of. No plane had ever been required to withstand the 500° to 1,000° F. temperatures generated by a constant speed of Mach 3. Aluminum was out of the question. It would not melt, but the heat would fatigue and weaken it. After consulting with metallurgists, Johnson settled on titanium—a heat-resistant metal that possesses the strength and heat resistance of steel, but is as light as aluminum.

When Lockheed began work on the A-12, titanium technology was in its infancy. The first titanium panels produced for the jet were so brittle that they shattered if dropped. As soon as that problem was solved, another arose that would have challenged Sherlock Holmes.

Skunk Works metallurgists found that the welds of some wing panels failed after only a short period of flight-simulation tests. Other panels seemed to last indefinitely. Sleuthing through production records, Johnson first discovered that panels welded during the summer had much shorter lives than those welded in winter. Further research revealed that the problem stemmed from the extra chlorine that Burbank used in its water system during the summer to prevent algae growth. When the welds were washed with the strongly chlorinated water, they weakened. Johnson ordered distilled water used in the process, and there were no more problems with weak welds.

Then, during heat tests, another problem developed. The wing panels warped so badly that they distorted the contour of the wing. Johnson decided to substitute corrugated panels that called to mind the skins of the Junkers and Ford trimotors of decades earlier. When the new panels were heated, the barely visible corrugations deepened a few thousandths of an inch, allowing the metal to expand without warping. The panels then returned to their basic shape as they cooled. "I was accused of trying to make a 1932 Ford Tri-Motor go Mach 3," Johnson recalled, "but the concept worked."

The plane's operating systems also had to work efficiently and reliably at high temperatures, and new products had to be created or improvised in several areas. A hydraulic fluid was developed to withstand temperatures of up to 650° F., 150° higher than the usual requirement. All electrical connections in the aircraft were gold-plated, since gold retains its electrical conductivity at high temperatures better than copper or silver. Control cables were made of Elgiloy, used in watch springs; an alloy of steel, chromium and nickel, it keeps its strength even when heated.

The engine selected to power Lockheed's new superplane was the

A Lockheed SR-71 Blackbird climbs above a cloud bank. The 107-foot-long jet's twin engines deliver a combined thrust of 65,000 pounds.

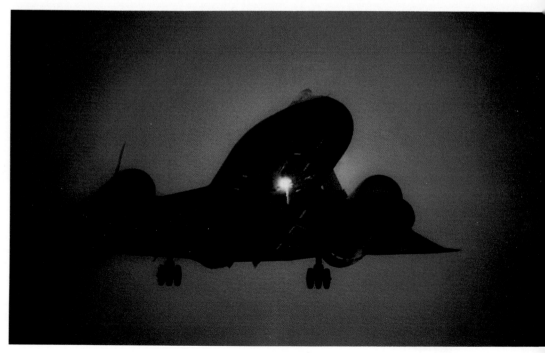

In this dramatic Air Force photograph, a Blackbird settles in for a landing at an air base in Louisiana. When the Mach 3 jet touches down, a large drag chute is deployed to help brake it.

This overhead view of an SR-71 highlights the craft's flared-out fuselage, designed to increase lift and stability.

Marked with a white cross to facilitate tracking, a Blackbird streaks toward a closed-course speed record of 2,193.2 mph in 1976.

Pratt & Whitney J58 turbojet. Originally designed for a Navy attack craft that never went into production, it had to be modified extensively to meet Johnson's demanding requirements. For example, in the A-12, the J58's afterburner would be used for hours on end instead of just a few minutes at a time. Yet the engine had to have low enough fuel consumption for the plane to fly more than 3,000 miles without refueling. In the end, only the engine's dimensions, and its turbine and compressor, remained unchanged.

Fueling the A-12 presented a thorny problem, one related to the construction of the plane. To save weight, the skin of the aircraft formed the walls of its fuel tanks. And because the skin would heat up dramatically during flight, then cool and contract afterward, it would be impossible to seal the fuselage completely against fuel leaks; on the ground, the A-12 would stand among small puddles of fuel that dripped slowly from the tanks. Fortunately, a jet fuel called JP-7 would be available for the A-12. With a flash point much higher than that of ordinary jet fuel, it could not be ignited by a stray spark or a match. This reluctance to burn meant that the JP-7 would have to be fired in the J58 engine by tetraethyl borane, a chemical so unstable that it ignites spontaneously in the open air. Fortunately, little of the liquid would be required, and it could be stored on the plane in a small, completely sealed tank.

The A-12 was pronounced ready for its first flight in the spring of 1962, while the J58 was still undergoing development. At that point, Johnson decided to equip the plane with less powerful J75 engines in order to try out its flight characteristics at low speeds. Lockheed test pilot Louis W. Schalk flew the underpowered A-12 several times. The plane performed as expected and Schalk experienced no difficulties.

Finally, in early 1963, the J58 engines were installed. Not all was rosy with the power plants. In early tests, Skunk Works engineers had difficulty accelerating the J58's compressor to starting speed, a problem Johnson solved by building a ground starter from two 300-horsepower Buick racing engines and coupling them through a common gearbox to spin the jet's compressor.

A movable cone in each of the A-12's air intakes helped control the supply of air to the engine. The cones were another source of trouble. During supersonic flight, the shock wave streaming back from the tip of the cone was supposed to remain within the air intake. But on occasion the shock wave popped out, suddenly depriving the engine of air. The accompanying loss of thrust was likened by test pilots to "being in a train wreck," as the aircraft decelerated suddenly and violently. To solve the problem, Pratt & Whitney engineers developed a system that automatically recaptured the shock wave so quickly that the pilot rarely could tell that an engine had failed. With the J58s operating reliably, the plane was ready to attempt Mach 3.

Sometime in mid-1963—many details about the flight remain secret—Schalk arrived one morning at the "Ranch," a heavily guarded test site in the southwestern United States. After conferring with flight

The star-crossed Valkyrie

In 1955, the U.S. Air Force laid plans for a supersonic nuclear bomber; the result in 1963 was the North American XB-70A Valkyrie, then the world's largest supersonic aircraft. It measured 105 feet from wing tip to wing tip and 189 feet from nose to tail along its gracefully arched fuselage.

With six General Electric YJ93 turbojets that produced more than 30,000 pounds of thrust apiece, the XB-70 was as fast as the Air Force had hoped. On October 14, 1965, a Valkyrie became the second jet-propelled aircraft, after the Lockheed Blackbird, to sustain a speed of Mach 3.

But by then, the plane had lost its luster as a superweapon—nuclear-tipped missiles were judged superior—and the idea for a fleet of Valkyries withered. The two prototypes continued as research craft, exploring problems encountered by large airplanes at supersonic speed. Then on June 8, 1966, one of the Valkyries was demolished in a midair collision *(overleaf)* with an F-104 Starfighter flown by Joe Walker, one of aviation's finest test pilots. Two years later, the research program was shelved as too costly, and the surviving XB-70 was retired to the Air Force Museum at Wright-Patterson Air Force Base, Ohio.

A crowd inspects the sleek lines of a Valkyrie XB-70 bomber at roll-out ceremonies on May 11, 1964.

The XB-70 leads a formation of supersonic jets seconds before Joe Walker's red-tailed F-104 collides with the bomber's right wing tip (opposite).

Trailing white plumes of fuel, the XB-70 begins to tumble earthward. Its pilot, Al White, managed to eject but was badly injured.

The doomed Valkyrie continues on course as Walker's F-104 explodes in flames; Walker had no chance to escape.

A plume of black smoke rises from the wreckage of the Valkyrie. The copilot, Carl Cross, went down with the plane.

operations personnel, Schalk was given a physical and helped to dress for the flight. Twenty minutes later he was fully encased, like a modern-day mummy, in a 40-pound pressure suit. The $100,000 ensemble—the gloves alone cost $2,000—might save his life if he had to eject at a high speed and altitude. Technicians connected him to a portable air-conditioning unit and drove him to the waiting A-12.

Once there, Schalk waddled awkwardly over to the plane and climbed a ladder to the cockpit. For nearly half an hour he and the ground crew ran through the aircraft's long preflight check list. Finally, the signal for ignition was given and the Buick engines began to spin the J58 turbines. The crew chief listened briefly to the rising whine of the engines; they sounded fine. He closed the plane's canopy and gave Schalk the thumbs-up sign.

As a chase plane trailed behind, Schalk steered the A-12 onto the runway, its nose bobbing slightly. When the control tower signaled all clear, Schalk advanced the throttles to full power. Twin flashes of orange exhaust cleaved the desert air as the afterburners cut in. The test pilot released the brakes and the A-12 trundled down the runway and shot into the air. Following a carefully planned scenario, Schalk climbed to about 35,000 feet, easily breaking Mach 1. He continued to climb and accelerate; within minutes he was flying at more than 2,000 miles an hour—Mach 3—at 70,000 feet. Before returning to base, Schalk eased the plane up another 10,000 feet.

Kelly Johnson's A-12 had met the challenge. The Air Force pronounced the plane fit for service and ordered an undisclosed number of an advanced two-seat model, designated the SR-71. President Lyndon Johnson announced the existence of the top-secret plane in February of 1964. The first SR-71s entered service with the Strategic Air Command two years later, inaugurating missions over Southeast Asia shortly thereafter. By then, the jet had acquired the nickname Blackbird; its titanium skin was painted black to enhance heat radiation from the plane and help cool it.

In 1974, a Blackbird set a transatlantic speed record of one hour 54 minutes and 56 seconds for the 3,470-mile route between New York and London—less than $1/17$ the time it had taken Charles Lindbergh to fly to Paris 45 years earlier. Two years later, the Blackbird set a world speed record for jets of 2,193.16 miles per hour.

Two decades after its first flight, the distinctively shaped Blackbird had yet to be surpassed; it represented the culmination of the great advances made in aviation since the days of biplanes. The creators of those fine craft were justly proud of simply getting into the air. They realized that the planes they built were limited, and the awareness compelled them to do better. Biplanes gave way to monoplanes, wooden construction to metal, piston engines to jets. And each leap forward attested to the questing spirit of aircraft designers and the courage of test pilots who, together, brought aviation from its horse-and-buggy days into the age of supersonic flight. ➤➤

Masterworks of the designer's art

When the General Dynamics F-111 *(below)* first flew in 1964, it represented a breakthrough in aircraft design. To be sure, it could fly neither as high nor as fast as Lockheed's SR-71 spy plane. But the fighter-bomber performed admirably in the role for which it was intended: It could take off from a runway only 3,500 feet long, streak to a target at more than twice the speed of sound, deliver its bombs, then dash back to base supersonically to rearm.

Behind the F-111's remarkable performance lay a feature that had never before appeared except on experimental aircraft—the swing wing. Anchored at pivots about halfway between nose and tail *(cutaway, overleaf),* the wings could be extended nearly straight out for taking off heavily loaded even from unpaved airstrips, then swept sharply back for supersonic flight.

By the early 1980s, designers had come up with many marvelous aircraft besides the F-111 and the SR-71. A few were little more than artists' preliminary sketches. Some were built for speed; some carried devastating weapons. Some flew high; others were agile. And some were designed mainly to be safe and enjoyable for weekend pilots. A gallery of these planes begins on page 164.

A camouflaged F-111, seen here with its wings almost fully extended, has just completed in-flight refueling. The F-111 had an unrefueled range of about 4,000 miles while carrying more than 24,000 pounds of bombs and missiles. Advanced radar and navigation systems allowed it to fly unescorted deep into enemy territory and make precision bombing runs at 1,200 mph "no matter how black the night," said one pilot, "or foul the weather."

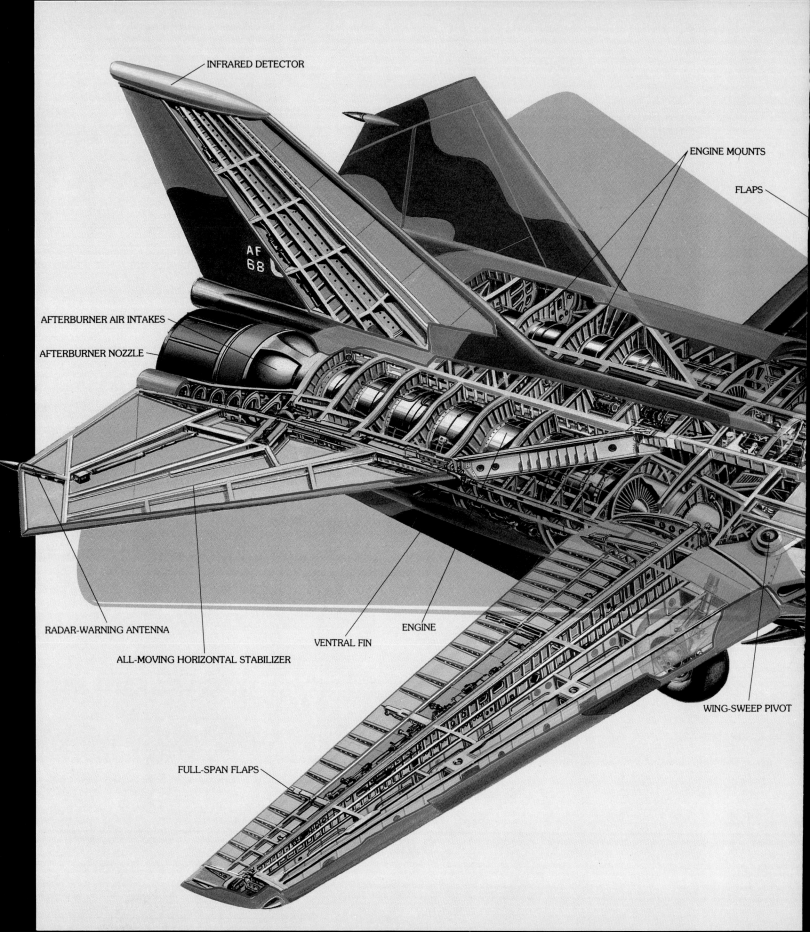

INFRARED DETECTOR

ENGINE MOUNTS

FLAPS

AF
68

AFTERBURNER AIR INTAKES

AFTERBURNER NOZZLE

RADAR-WARNING ANTENNA

ENGINE

VENTRAL FIN

ALL-MOVING HORIZONTAL STABILIZER

WING-SWEEP PIVOT

FULL-SPAN FLAPS

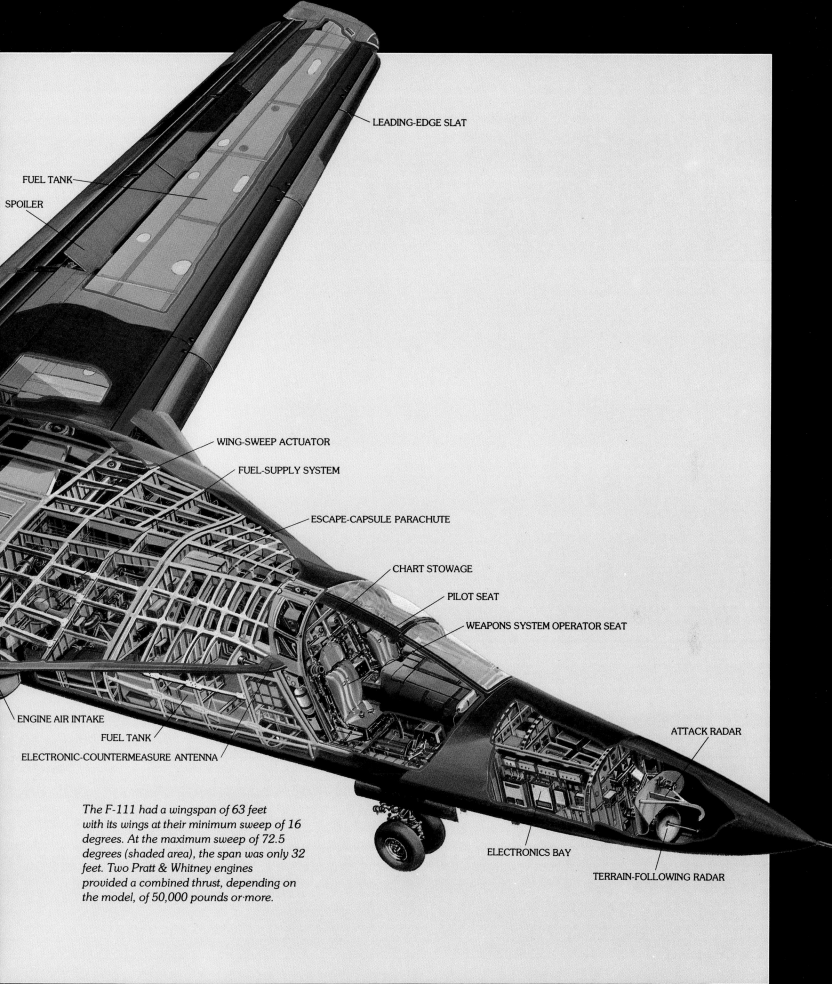

LEADING-EDGE SLAT

FUEL TANK

SPOILER

WING-SWEEP ACTUATOR

FUEL-SUPPLY SYSTEM

ESCAPE-CAPSULE PARACHUTE

CHART STOWAGE

PILOT SEAT

WEAPONS SYSTEM OPERATOR SEAT

ENGINE AIR INTAKE

FUEL TANK

ELECTRONIC-COUNTERMEASURE ANTENNA

ATTACK RADAR

ELECTRONICS BAY

TERRAIN-FOLLOWING RADAR

The F-111 had a wingspan of 63 feet with its wings at their minimum sweep of 16 degrees. At the maximum sweep of 72.5 degrees (shaded area), the span was only 32 feet. Two Pratt & Whitney engines provided a combined thrust, depending on the model, of 50,000 pounds or·more.

The General Dynamics F-16XL differs from the F-16 mainly in its new cranked-arrow wing, named for its zigzag leading edge. This wing cuts drag 53 per cent and contains large fuel tanks. Together these features allow the F-16XL to fly half again as far as the F-16 while carrying twice the payload.

A HiMAT (Highly Maneuverable Aircraft Technology) radio-controlled drone, built by Rockwell International, banks into a turn over California. This plane, with wing and tail modules for testing a variety of airfoil shapes, cost less than one fourth the price of a manned aircraft of the same versatility.

The navigation lights of a McDonnell Douglas advanced version of the British Aerospace Harrier trace the plane's corkscrew descent in this time-exposure photograph of a nighttime landing. The jet's engine is equipped with exhaust nozzles that swivel for vertical takeoffs and landings.

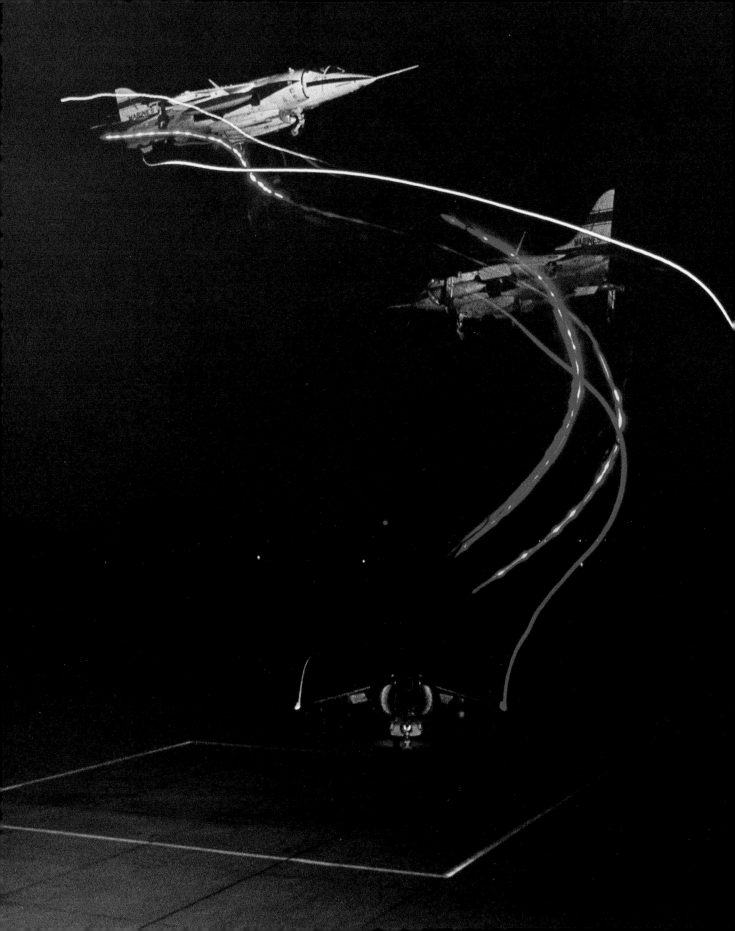

Nose lowered to give the pilot a view of
the runway, a prototype of the Anglo-French
Concorde supersonic transport takes off
on its maiden flight in 1969. The Mach 2.2
jet, which seats 100 and has a range of
3,050 miles, was subjected to a series of
extremely rigorous flight tests and did not
enter service until 1975.

The Bell XV-15 tilts its engines from vertical
to horizontal during a test flight. With its
rotors pointed up, the experimental craft can
hover, land or take off like a helicopter;
with its rotors pointed forward, the XV-15
performs like a conventional airplane

The rocket-powered Martin-Marietta
X-24B research plane glides to earth during
a 1970s test flight. The wingless craft
is referred to as a lifting body because
the fuselage provides lift.

Mated to a huge fuel tank and two booster
rockets, space shuttle Columbia, the world's
first reusable spacecraft, stands poised
for launch at Cape Canaveral. The shuttle,
which is designed to carry a payload into
orbit and return, took off on April 12, 1981,
and two days later glided to a perfect landing
at Edwards Air Force Base, California.

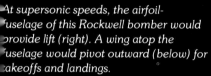

A delta-winged bomber proposed by Rockwell International is a span loader—it would carry its entire payload inside the wing. The plane is illustrated here destroying an enemy missile with a laser beam.

At supersonic speeds, the airfoil-fuselage of this Rockwell bomber would provide lift (right). A wing atop the fuselage would pivot outward (below) for takeoffs and landings.

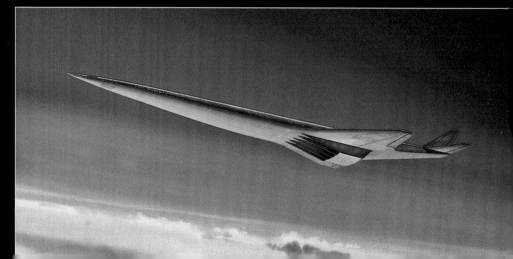

Lockheed's 21st Century Mach 4 airliner would carry an estimated 200 passengers at an altitude of 120,000 feet.

Proposed as a missile-launching platform, this Boeing turboprop would have exceptionally low fuel consumption. It features efficient propellers with thin blades and tips that are swept to reduce drag.

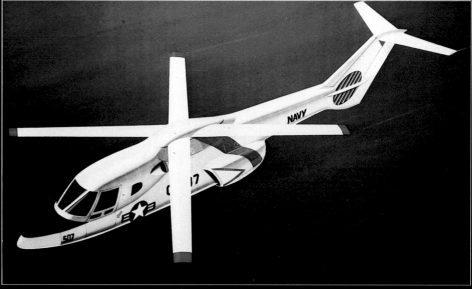

The rotor of this jet-powered helicopter proposed for the U.S. Navy would be immobilized after takeoff to serve as an X-shaped wing for high-speed flight.

This gigantic Lockheed air freighter, a span loader like the Rockwell bomber on the opposite page, has a 252-foot wing that could hold 600,000 pounds of cargo. The plane would have a range of 5,000 miles.

Acknowledgments

The index for this book was prepared by Gale Linck Partoyan. For their help in the preparation of this volume, the editors wish to thank: **In France:** Le Bourget—Georges Delaleau, Yvan Kayser, Général Pierre Lissarague, Director, Jean-Yves Lorent, Général Roger de Ruffray, Deputy-Director, Colonel Pierre Willefert, Curator, Musée de l'Air; Paris—Avions Marcel Dassault-Breguet Aviation, Colonel Edmond Petit, Curator, Musée Air-France; Robert Roux, G.I.F.A.S. **In the Federal Republic of Germany:** Berlin (West)—Dr. Roland Klemig, Heidi Klein, Bildarchiv Preussischer Kulturbesitz; Wolfgang Streubel, Ullstein Bilderdienst; Munich—Hans Ebert, Messerschmitt-Bölkow-Blohm; Kyril von Gersdorff, Walter Zucker, Deutsches Museum; Swistall-Buschhoven—Ernst M. Paulsen; Wentorf/Hamburg—Kurt Reitsch. **In the German Democratic Republic:** Berlin (DDR)—Hannes Quaschinsky, ADN-Zentralbild. **In Great Britain:** Cambridge—Constance Babington-Smith; Farnborough—D. W. Goode, B. C. Kervell, Royal Aircraft Establishment; London—John Bagley, Science Museum; Arnold Nayler, Royal Aeronautical Society; Bruce Robertson; Marjorie Willis, BBC Hulton Picture Library; Surrey—E. B. Morgan; West Midlands—Michael Daunt. **In Italy:** Milan—Maurizio Pagliano; Rome—Contessa Maria Fede Caproni, Museo Aeronautico Caproni di Taliedo; Cesare Falessi, Aeritalia; Capitano Mario Manca, Stato Maggiore Aeronautica. **In the United States:** California—Dr. Ira E. Chart, Historian, Aircraft Division, Northrop Corporation; Peter Ferguson, Public Information Coordinator, Lockheed-California Company; Harry S. Gann, Manager, Bruce MacKenzie, Aircraft Information, Douglas Aircraft Company; Edward Heinemann; Jerome Lederer; Anthony Le Vier; Chere Negaard, Library Director, Northrop University Library; Glenn E. Odekirk; Ben Rich, Vice-President and General Manager, Advanced Development Projects, Lockheed Corporation; John Underwood; Washington, D.C.—Bob Dreesen, Phil Edwards, National Air and Space Museum Library; Julie Gustafson, Susan E. Simpson, Researchers, Defense Audio Visual Agency; E. T. Wooldridge Jr., Curator for Aeronautics, National Air and Space Museum; Texas—Paul Bailey, Research Associate, Hoblitzelle Theatre Arts Library, Humanities Research Center, the University of Texas at Austin; Virginia—Scott Crossfield; Moses Farmer, Aerospace Engineer, Charlie M. Jackson Jr., Director, Supersonic Aerodynamics Branch, Richard Layman, Langley Historical Program Coordinator, Pat Zoeller, Public Affairs, NASA Langley Research Center; Lieutenant Colonel Eric M. Solander, Chief, Magazines and Books Division, First Lieutenant Peter S. Meltzer Jr., Deputy Chief, U.S. Air Force Office of Public Affairs. A particularly useful source of information and quotations for this volume was *Revolution in the Sky: Those Fabulous Lockheeds and the Pilots Who Flew Them* by Richard Sanders Allen, the Stephen Greene Press, 1967.

Picture credits

Bibliography

Books

Allen, James Ross, *Aerodynamics and Flight.* International Textbook, 1935.

Allen, Richard Sanders, *Revolution in the Sky: Those Fabulous Lockheeds and the Pilots Who Flew Them.* The Stephen Greene Press, 1967.

Anderson, Fred, *Northrop: An Aeronautical History.* Northrop Corporation, 1976.

Avions Marcel Dassault-Breguet Aviation: From Ouragan to Super Mirage 4000. Avions Marcel Dassault-Breguet Aviation, 1979.

Babington-Smith, Constance, *Testing Time: The Story of British Test Pilots and Their Aircraft.* Harper & Brothers, 1961.

Bowyer, Chaz, *Mosquito at War.* Charles Scribner's Sons, 1973.

Boyne, Walter J., and Donald S. Lopez, *The Jet Age: Forty Years of Jet Aviation.* National Air and Space Museum, Smithsonian Institution, 1979.

Bridgman, Leonard, ed., *Jane's All The World's Aircraft 1945-1946.* Arco, 1977.

Conradis, Heinz, *Design for Flight: The Kurt Tank Story.* Transl. by Kenneth Kettle. London: MacDonald, 1960.

Craig, James F., *Famous Aircraft: The Messerschmitt Bf.109.* Arco, 1968.

Crossfield, A. Scott, with Clay Blair Jr., *Always Another Dawn: The Story of a Rocket Test Pilot.* Arno Press, 1972.

De Havilland, Sir Geoffrey, *Sky Fever.* Shrewsbury, England: Airlife, 1979.

Fokker, Anthony H. G., and Bruce Gould, *Flying Dutchman: The Life of Anthony Fokker.* Arno Press, 1972.

Fowler, Harlan D., *Fowler Flaps for Airplanes: An Engineering Handbook.* Wetzel, 1948.

Foxworth, Thomas G., *The Speed Seekers.* Doubleday, 1974.

Francillon, René J., *McDonnell Douglas Aircraft since 1920.* London: Putnam, 1979.

Gibbs-Smith, Charles Harvard:
The Aeroplane: An Historical Survey of Its Origins and Development. London: Her Majesty's Stationery Office, 1960.
The Invention of the Aeroplane (1799-1909). Taplinger, 1965.

Glines, Carroll V., and Wendell F. Moseley, *The Legendary DC-3.* Van Nostrand Reinhold, 1979.

Gray, George W., *Frontiers of Flight: The Story of NACA Research.* Alfred A. Knopf, 1948.

Green, William:
Famous Fighters of the Second World War. Hanover House, 1957.
The Warplanes of the Third Reich. Doubleday, 1970.

Gunston, Bill:
Classic Aircraft Fighters. Grosset & Dunlap, 1978.
Early Supersonic Fighters of the West. Charles Scribner's Sons, 1976.
The Illustrated Encyclopedia of the World's Modern Military Aircraft. Salamander Books, 1977.

Gurney, Gene, ed., *Test Pilots.* Franklin Watts, 1962.

Hallion, Richard P., *Test Pilots: The Frontiersmen of Flight.* Doubleday, 1981.

Hallion, Richard P., ed., *The Wright Brothers: Heirs of Prometheus.* National Air and Space Museum, Smithsonian Institution, 1978.

Harker, Ronald W., *The Engines Were Rolls-Royce: An Informal History of That Famous Company.* Macmillan, 1979.

Hegener, Henri, *Fokker: The Man and His Aircraft.* Letchworth, England: Harleyford, 1961.

Holland, Maurice, with Thomas M. Smith, *Architects of Aviation.* Duell, Sloan and Pearce, 1951.

Ingells, Douglas J.:
The McDonnell Douglas Story. Aero, 1979.
The Plane that Changed the World: A Biography of the DC-3. Aero, no date.

Keats, John, *Howard Hughes.* Random House, 1966.

Kennode, Alfred Coterill, *Mechanics of Flight.* Pitman, 1972.

Kinert, Reed, *Racing Planes and Air Races, a Complete History,* Vol. 3. Aero, 1969.

Knaack, Marcelle Size, *Encyclopedia of U.S. Air Force Aircraft and Missile Systems,* Vol. 1. Office of Air Force History, 1978.

Lewis, Peter, *British Aircraft 1809-1914.* London: Putnam, 1962.

Lockheed Aircraft Corporation, *Lockheed's Family Tree: A History of the Company's Early Aircraft.* Lockheed Aircraft, 1978.

Ludington, Charles Townsend, *Smoke Streams: Visualized Air Flow.* Coward-McCann, 1943.

Mason, Francis K., *Harrier.* Naval Institute Press, 1981.

Matt, Paul R., with Thomas G. Foxworth, Ken C. Rust, eds., *Historical Aviation Album, All American Series,* Vol. 16. Historical Aviation Album, 1980.

Maynard, Crosby, *Flight Plan for Tomorrow: The Douglas Story, a Condensed History.* Douglas Aircraft, 1966.

Miller, Ronald E., and David Sawers, *The Technical Development of Modern Aviation.* London: Routledge & Kegan Paul, 1968.

Mohler, Stanley R., and Bobby H. Johnson, *Wiley Post, His Winnie Mae, and the World's First Pressure Suit.* Smithsonian Institution Press, 1971.

Munson, Kenneth:
Airliners between the Wars 1919-1939. Macmillan, 1972.
German Aircraft of World War 2. Poole, England: Blandford Press, 1978.
Pioneer Aircraft 1903-1914. Macmillan, 1969.

Nayler, J. L., and E. Ower, *Aviation: Its Technical Development.* Dufour Editions, 1965.

Nowarra, Heinz J.:
The Focke-Wulf 190: Famous German Fighter. Aero, 1965.
The Messerschmitt 109: A Famous German Fighter. Aero, 1963.

Odekirk, Glenn, *HK-1 Hercules: A Pictorial History of the Fantastic Hughes Flying Boat.* Fragments West, 1982.

Pendray, G. Edward, ed., *The Guggenheim Medalists: Architects of the Age of Flight.* The Guggenheim Medal Board of Award, 1964.

Perry, Robert, *A Dassault Dossier: Aircraft Acquisition in France.* The Rand Corporation, 1973.

Petit, Edmond, *Nouvelle Histoire Mondiale de l'Aviation.* Paris: Librairie Hachette, 1973.

Pope, Alan, *Aerodynamics of Supersonic Flight: An Introduction.* Pitman, 1950.

Randers-Pherson, Nils Henrik, *Pioneer Wind Tunnels.* The Smithsonian Institution, 1935.

Reitsch, Hanna, *Flying Is My Life.* Transl. by Lawrence Wilson, G. P. Putnam's Sons, 1954.

Schlaifer, Robert, and S. D. Heron, *Development of Aircraft Engines* and *Development of Aviation Fuels.* Division of Research, Graduate School of Business Administration, Harvard University, 1950.

Shapiro, Ascher H., *Shape and Flow: The Fluid Dynamics of Drag.* Doubleday, 1961.

The Society of Experimental Test Pilots, *1975 Report to the Aerospace Profession, Nineteenth Symposium Proceedings,* 1975.

Spenser, Jay P., *Bellanca C.F.: The Emergence of the Cabin Monoplane in the United States.* Smithsonian Institution Press, 1982.

Stephens, Moye W., "Whither the Wild Blue Yonder?" Manuscript, no date.

Talay, Theodore A., *Introduction to the Aerodynamics of Flight.* National Aeronautics and Space Administration, 1975.

Tantum, W. H., and E. J. Hoffschmidt, eds., *The Rise and Fall of the German Air Force.* WE Inc., 1969.

Taylor, C. Fayette, *Aircraft Propulsion: A Review of Aircraft Piston Engines.* Smithsonian Institution, 1971.

Taylor, Michael J. H., *Jane's Pocket Book of Research and Experimental Aircraft.* Macmillan, 1976.

United States National Aeronautics and Space Administration:
Technical Facilities Catalog, Vol. 1, 1974.
Wind Tunnels of NASA. No date.

United States Navy, Bureau of Aeronautics, Training Division, *Principles of Flying.* McGraw-Hill, 1943.

Vader, John, *Spitfire.* Ballantine Books, 1969.

Van Ishoven, Armand:
Messerschmitt: Aircraft Designer. Doubleday, 1975.
Messerschmitt Bf 109 at War. Charles Scribner's Sons, 1977.

Vickers-Armstrong Limited, *Supermarine Spitfire: 40th Anniversary.* 1976.

Villard, Henry Serrano, *Contact! The Story of the Early Birds.* Bonanza Books, 1968.

Von Kármán, Theodore, *Aerodynamics.* Cornell University Press, 1954.

Wagner, Ray, *American Combat Planes.* Doubleday, 1982.

Welbourne, G. V., *Flight and Engines.* London: Blackie & Son, 1945.

Weyl, A. R., *Fokker: The Creative Years.* London: Putnam, 1965.

Whittle, Sir Frank, *Jet: The Story of a Pioneer.* London: Frederick Muller, 1953.

Wolfe, Tom, *The Right Stuff.* Bantam Books, 1979.

Wolko, Howard S., *In the Cause of Flight: Technologists of Aeronautics and Astronautics.* Smithsonian Institution Press, 1981.

Wooldridge, E. T., Jr., *The P-80 Shooting Star, Evolution of a Jet Fighter.* Smithsonian Institution Press, 1979.

Periodicals

Johnson, Clarence L., "Development of the Lockheed SR-71 Blackbird." *Lockheed Horizons,* Winter 1981/82.

Saar, John, "New Wind Tunnels Shape the Future." *Smithsonian,* January 1982.

Index